GW01219726

ELM PARK
1626-1954

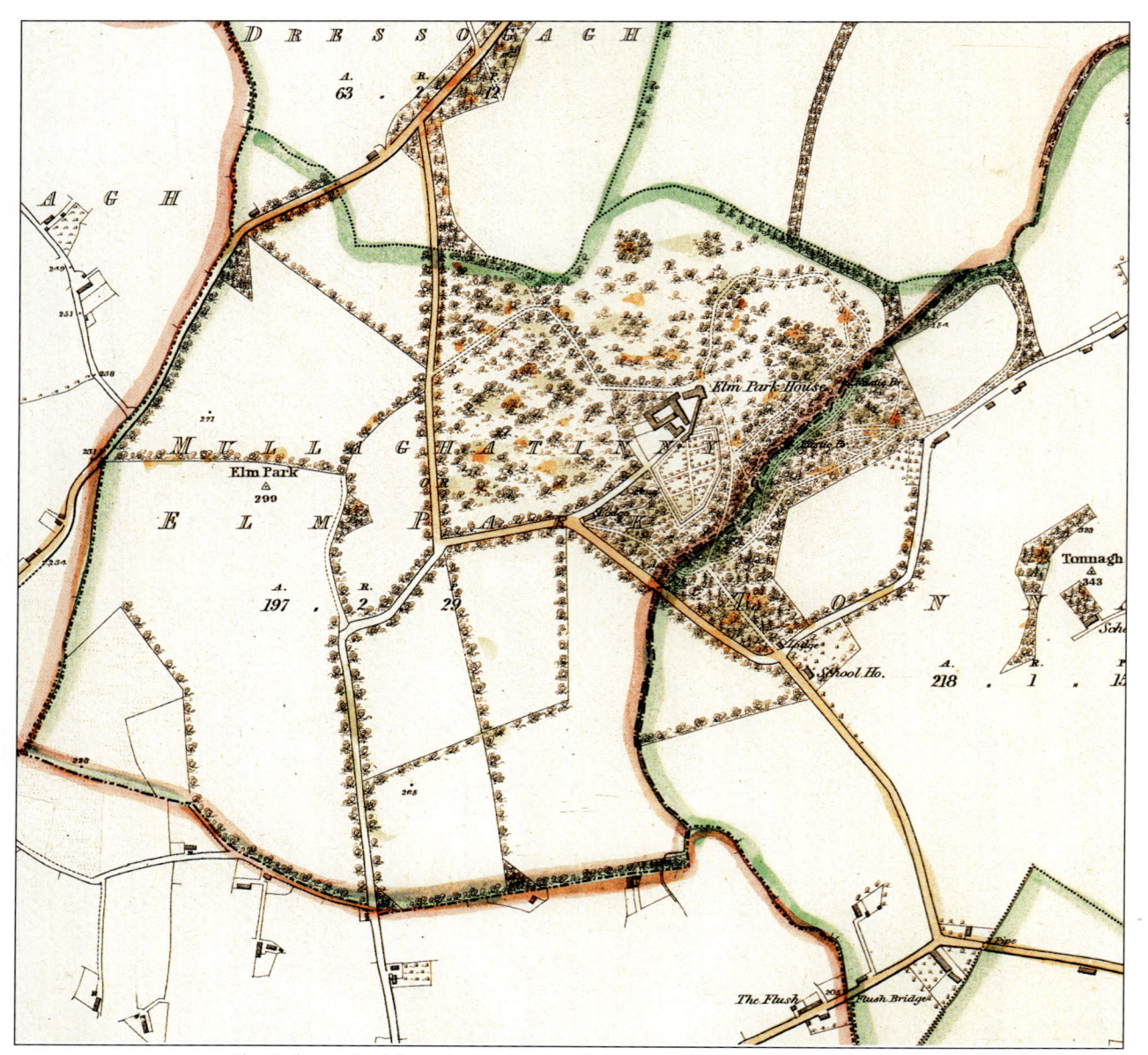

Elm Park townland from the 6 inch = 1 mile Ordnance Survey map, 1835 edition.

ELM PARK
1626-1954

COUNTRY HOUSE TO PREPARATORY SCHOOL

SEAN BARDEN

ULSTER HISTORICAL
FOUNDATION

Ulster Historical Foundation is pleased to acknowledge the support of
Armagh City and District Council
The Esme Mitchell Trust
The Miss Elizabeth Ellison Charitable Trust
Ulster Garden Villages Ltd
and
all subscribers and donors
whose assistance has made the publication of this book possible.

First published in 2004
by Ulster Historical Foundation
12 College Square East, Belfast, BT1 6DD
www.ancestryireland.com
www.booksireland.org.uk

Except as otherwise permitted under the Copyright, Designs and Patents Act 1988, this publication may only be reproduced, stored or transmitted in any form or by any means with the prior permission in writing of the publisher or, in the case of reprographic reproduction, in accordance with the terms of a licence issued by The Copyright Licensing Agency. Enquiries concerning reproduction outside those terms should be sent to the publisher.

© Sean Barden, 2004

Printed by ColourBooks Ltd
Design by December Publications

ISBN 1-903688-42-6

South elevation of Elm Park House, from drawings by J. Rawson Carroll.
Reproduced with the permission of the Armagh County Museum/MAGNI.

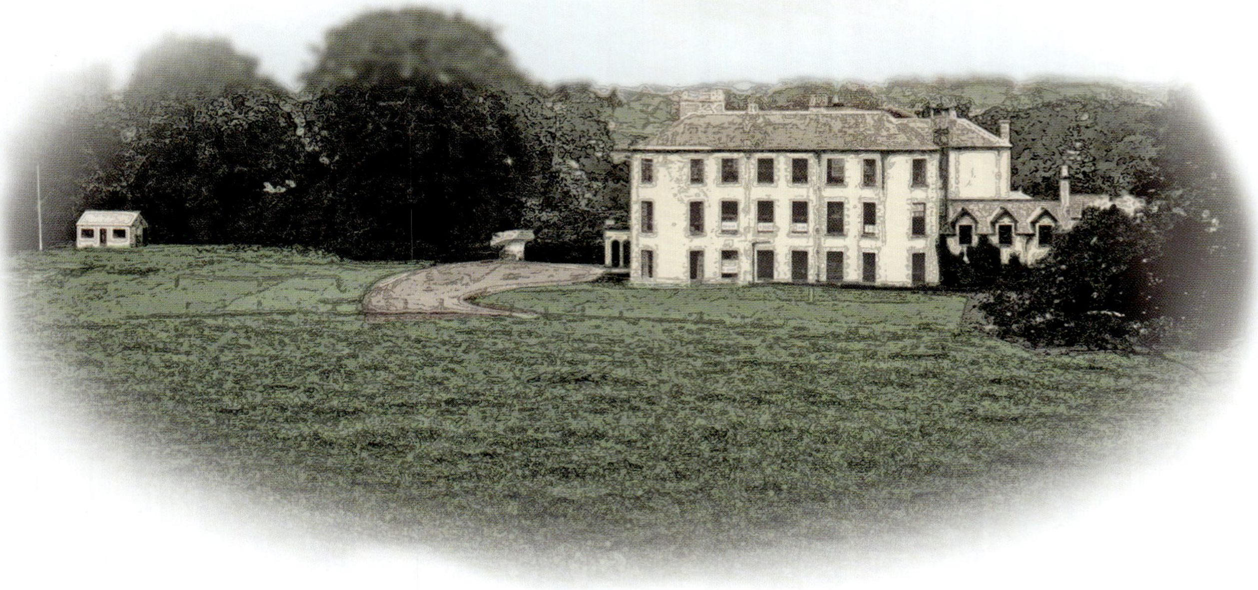

CONTENTS

Foreword	ix
Preface	xi
List of subscribers	xiii
Introduction: Prep schools	1
Elm Park House: the estate and its history	4
Elm Park School	21
The founders	22
Integration	29
The school day	33
Comings and goings	38
Organised entertainment	43
Organised sport	47
The Glen	53
Home comforts, food and health	59
Food	59
Sickness	63
Chilly weather	65
Academic standards	67
Teaching staff	71
Headmasters	71
Teachers	71
Woodwork, art and music	74
Non-teaching staff	84
Matrons	84
Household and outdoor staff	85
After Elm Park	87
Chronological summary	90
Elm Park today	97
Appendices	99
Bibliography	129
Index	133

VIRTUTE ET CONSTANTIA

FOREWORD

It had been acknowledged for some time that a record should be written about Elm Park School but this did not appear likely to materialise. The reunions of 1975, 1995 and 2001 took place without anything definite being put in place. Indeed, at the 2001 meeting, I went as far as saying that as no plans were in place at least all the material that could be gathered should be deposited in the Public Record Office of Northern Ireland.

After the last reunion I was made aware of a potential author, Sean Barden, who had recently produced a small, well researched and written booklet relating to the last Countess Charlemont. I arranged to introduce myself and was very surprised to find that there was enthusiasm for the concept despite the fact that he knew nothing about the school. However, since he worked in Armagh County Museum, he had acquired a knowledge of a number of the important local families. He readily undertook the task of writing an account of 'the Estate House and the families connected with it' and the school up to the time that it closed in 1954.

I undertook to attend to the arrangements relating to publisher, funding and other matters. My appeal for subscribers resulted in an excellent response from almost one hundred Old Boys. Fintan Mullan, Executive Director, Ulster Historical Foundation, provisionally agreed to publish and obtain financial support from a number of charities. It soon became evident that the resources to carry forward the project were falling into place.

Sean Barden acknowledges elsewhere the extensive help given to him by the 'Old Boys' and others to enable him, over months of hard work and research, to produce this publication. The Curator and staff at Armagh County Museum have been very supportive. I gratefully acknowledge the help given by Dr W.H. Crawford and the support of Dr Kathleen Rankin, especially in the earlier years in getting the project underway. If you judge this book by the cover, greatly enhanced by a photographic expert friend of mine, Alan Ellison, I am sure that you will find the content matches it and does justice to the founders of this extraordinary school.

John R. Cowdy

PREFACE

The first thing to point out about this book is that it is divided into two very distinct parts which, although complementing each other can, be treated independently. The foremost intention is to tell the story of Elm Park School which flourished from 1921 to 1954. However the house in which the school was established had a long history going back centuries. It was the home in turn of the Maxwell, Close and Blacker families and the first part of the book traces their connection with the house and Elm Park townland. The vicissitudes of the house and demesne weave their way through a series of marriages and inheritances from the Plantation to the early twentieth century. It is a fascinating if at times complex insight into the personalities concerned and their relationship with each other and the surrounding area.

The second half of the book concentrates on the school itself, looking at the boys and staff who came and went through its doors during its thirty-three years. It is not a strict chronological account by any means; that rigorously linear approach would not do justice to the school or give a proper impression of Elm Park. Instead I have aimed to build from what facts, figures and anecdotes I have gathered, an impression of the character and spirit of the school. Some of the drier factual material is consigned to appendices but can be easily accessed.

Much of the main body of the text is based on the memories of those who attended the school. Over forty old boys responded to a questionnaire, providing invaluable information that I have used extensively. To respect the anonymity of the information they provided, I rarely mention them by name. To them and all the people who have helped I must express my thanks. The following is a list of those who kindly provided me with so much useful and personal insight to their school and school days. Many of them also supplied photographs which bring to life their anecdotes and memories. They are: Peter Acheson, Allen Anderson, Henry Armstrong, John Baxter, Robert Bell, Henry Blood-Smyth, Michael Burges, Garry Campbell, Derek Carr, Jimmy Carr, Robin Charley, Henry Clark, John Cowdy, Ralph Cowdy, Malcolm Crawford, Adrian Forrest, Robin Graham, Tim Herdman, Robin Hill, Peter Hinchcliffe, David Hobday, Patrick Horsbrugh, Bill Jackson, Mervyn Knox-Brown, James Leslie, Finlay McCance, Neill McCance, Angus McConnell, Shean McConnell, Dick McDonald, Donald MacLeay, William McMullan, Robert Magill, David Maxwell, Hugh Montgomery, Bill Moore, Dick Perceval-Maxwell, Tim Sinton, Harry Stevenson, Charlie Stewart, John Stewart, Ian Stoupe, David Strachan, Jackson Taggart,

Michael Topping, David Trustram-Eve (Lord Silsoe), Peter Trustram-Eve, Cyril Ward and Desmond Woods.

However it was to John Cowdy whose idea this project was, that I turned most often with all sorts of questions and I must thank him especially for going to so much time and effort to provide the answers. I must also thank him for introducing me to the absorbing world of Elm Park when he asked me to embark on this project almost eighteen months ago. It has been a fascinating journey. John's own substantial archive of Elm Park documents and photographs was complemented by the wealth of material and personal memories provided by former headmaster Michael Williams. Without this valuable information the book would have been impossible. Michael's deep and thorough knowledge of prep schools was also of great help to me. The help and guidance provided by Dr Bill Crawford was crucial to this whole project. He not only made many and valuable suggestions that improved the structure of the text but encouraged me whenever he could.

I must also thank the institutions and archives I used and which provided source material. Firstly the Curator of Armagh County Museum, Catherine McCullough, for her constant help and for making freely available the writings of T.G.F. Paterson held there. They were invaluable for building up a picture of the early history, as was the newspaper archive held by the Irish and Local Studies Library in Armagh. Mary McVeigh, the librarian at that institution, and all the staff of the library were always helpful. The staff at the Public Record Office of Northern Ireland must also be thanked together with all the people who provided photographs, letters and documents which went to help build a picture of Elm Park School even if they were not all eventually used in the book.

There were so many specialists in architecture, education and other areas who provided valuable help and support throughout the project, and of course the archivists from various public schools, who all gave freely of their valuable time to listen and answer my questions. They are Robin Allport, Molly Barton, Hannah Betts, Elizabeth Boardman, Joanne Bowley, Ben Cahill, Robin Charley, Mrs Dorothy Cowdy, Sue Croucher, J.A.K. Dean, Jason Diamond, Allan Ellison, Mrs Diana Faure-Walker (née Seth-Smith), Janey Goodard, Chris Gosnell, Kathy Gourlay, John E. Grant, Jonathan Hamill, Kisstine Hogg, Nigel Horsfall, Paul Larmour, Lauren Leason, Walter MacAulay, Tony Merrick, Kay Muhr, Elaine Mundill, Norman Nicholl, Miceal O'Mainain, Richard Oram, George Preston, Fred Rankin, Dr Kathleen Rankin, Penny Redman, Terence Reeves-Smith, Cmdr Martin Seth-Smith, Jackie Smith, Ernest Speers, Mervyn Speers, Andrew Stephen, William Trevor, Linda Wasson and Roger Weatherup. A special thanks to my wife Pauline and my children Alex and Louise for putting up with me throughout the project.

Sean Barden

LIST OF SUBSCRIBERS

Peter Acheson	Teddy Graham	Bill Moore
Michael Adeley	Simon Haselden	Robert Morton
Allen Anderson	Mark Herdman	William Mullan
John Andrews	Tim Herdman	Eddie Orr
Henry Armstrong	Robin Hill	Philip Orr
John Baxter	Peter Hinchcliffe	Terrance Patterson-Moutray
Robert Bell	David Hobday	Michael Perceval-Maxwell
Edward Bird	Jeremy Hughes	Richard Perceval-Maxwell
Henry Blood-Smyth	Bill Jackson	John Pringle
Michael Burges	David Kingan	Martin Proctor
Franklin Cardy	Alan Knighton Smith	Robin Sadlier
Derek Carr	Mervyn Knox-Brown	Nicholas Sholto-Cooke
Jimmy Carr	John Leslie	Tim Sinton
Alan Carson	Jeremy Lowndes (donation)	Harry Stevenson
Robin Charley	Finlay McCance	Charles Stewart
Henry Clark	Neill McCance	John Stewart
Christopher Cowdy	Angus McConnell	Colin Stoupe
John R. Cowdy	Don McConnell	Ian Stoupe
Ralph Cowdy	Shean McConnell	David Strachan
Roly Cunningham	Dick McDonald	John Swiney
Sam Cunningham	Malcolm McGregor	Andrew Topping
Stephen Dickson	Donald MacLeay	Michael Topping
Tom Dickson	David McManus	Peter Trustram-Eve
Arthur Douglas-Nugent	Lewis Maitland-Titterton	David Trustram-Eve
Norman Ferguson	David Maxwell	Ian Wilson
Alexander Fforde	Richard Millar	
John Fisher	John Miller (donation)	
Adrian Forrest	Bill Montgomery	
Owen French	Hugh Montgomery	Mrs Margaret Adair
Stanley Good	Ion Montgomery	Dorinda, Lady Dunleath
Michael Gordon	Patrick Montgomery	Lady Lucy Faulkner

School of 1950

Back Row: G. Beatty, Bill Jackson, Philip Orr, Ralph Cowdy, John Swiney, John Chambre, Anthony Orr, Michael Gordon, Tony Wilkinson, Michael Mackinnon, Edward Bird, David Lee, Michael Boyne, Corry Caruth, Alan Carson.

Second Row: Jackson Taggart, John Baxter, Don McConnell, Alastair Perceval-Maxwell, William Mullan, John Burrell, Michael Topping, Roger Austin, Bobby Boulton, David McMullan, John Russell, Ian Stoupe, George Fulton.

Front Row: Simon Haselden, Peter Acheson, Mr G.D. Lowdall, Miss Burrowes, Mrs Brown, Mr Willoughby Weaving, Mr Michael Valentine Rowley Williams, Mrs M.V.R. Williams, Miss McQuaide, Mr N. Nicholl, John Graham, David Strachan.

Seated on ground: David Montgomery, William Brodie.

INTRODUCTION
PREP SCHOOLS

Prep schools were boarding schools established in the countryside to segregate and cater for boys between the ages of seven and fourteen who were destined for education in institutions largely concerned with the teaching of the classics.

In England the preparatory school can trace its origins back to the early nineteenth century and even further in the form of such precursors as rectory schools and private classical schools. Like the larger and longer established public schools these early minor establishments prepared boys for a classical education at university. By the latter half of the century however, many of these minor, mostly country schools, had stopped competing with the public schools, tending to concentrate instead on educating younger boys. They became feeders for the public schools. This role was emphasised after 1864 when a parliamentary report recommended that it was not only beneficial but also desirable to educate younger boys separately and thus prepare them for the rigours of public school in the distinctive environment of the developing preparatory school system.

During the following decades several public schools raised the age at which they accepted boys, thus creating an even greater demand for prep schools. Prep schools in turn were very much influenced by the subjects taught in public schools and especially the subjects tested in scholarship examinations. By the 1890s when most younger boys were educated separately, it was a natural progression that the public schools should set their own entrance examinations.

By the end of the nineteenth century the prep schools had developed from a disparate scatter of individual small schools to such an extent that in 1892 an Association of Headmasters of Preparatory Schools was formed to make relations between prep schools and public schools closer and more systematic. By 1904 the Association had instigated the first Common Entrance Examinations, getting rid of the confusion of widely differing entrance exams in different schools.

By the time Elm Park was founded in 1921 the template from which prep schools was conceived was well established and widespread. Mourne Grange in County Down had been founded in 1900 and, together with a few other contenders, claims the distinction of being the first prep school in Ireland. As by that date prep schools in England had reached quite a mature stage in their evolution, it is obvious that prep schools in Ireland were late developers.

ELM PARK: COUNTRY HOUSE TO PREPARATORY SCHOOL

The establishment of schools in Ireland on English lines can be traced back to the reign of King Henry VIII but the first schools that functioned were the Diocesan Schools founded by an act of Queen Elizabeth I. Later the Royal Free Schools planned by King James I in conjunction with the Plantation of Ulster at the start of the seventeenth century enjoyed a longer lasting success. It is not known yet how closely the Royal Schools resembled English public schools but they did reflect something of the larger English institutions. In 1835 the headmaster of Armagh Royal stated that the 'school course ... was taken from that observed at Eton but modified to the course required at Trinity College Dublin'. Even if the curriculum was similar, however, it had to be admitted that Armagh Royal School was then a very modest establishment with only thirty-six students.

The whole question of the existence and evolution in Ireland of classical schools similar to the public schools in England awaits research. As early as 1835 a House of Commons committee reported about Diocesan Schools: 'It is not generally understood whether they are designed for gratuitous education and open to all persuasions or are classical boarding schools preparatory to the university, principally intended for the upper classes'. A perception existed that Diocesan Schools functioned to educate the sons of the clergy and professionals.

Prep schools like Mourne Grange and Rockport that emerged in the north of Ireland at the beginning of the twentieth century do not seem to have evolved from native institutions but were created to meet a different need. Their role was to prepare boys to attend English public schools as well as local equivalents such as Campbell College in Belfast and St. Columba's outside Dublin. In almost every sense except location these schools were typical English schools.

When we examine Elm Park in detail, it will become apparent just how much of an English institution it was. The remarkable description below of an imaginary archetypical English prep school taken from James Kenward's book *Prep School*, published in 1958, could easily be a bird's eye view of Elm Park:

> In imagination I see it from the air, a stolid Georgian house approached by a wide and winding drive, with fir trees on the lawn, with shrubberies, with a walled kitchen garden and outbuildings galore. Beyond are meadows, the nearest to the house being the playing field. Beyond again is the undulating English countryside.
>
> Turning my back to the house I see the drive leading into the lane that passes by on its way to the village, then the road setting out towards the town that is visited on special occasions; and as I look a white feather of steam appears, marking the railway station, the departure and arrival port to and from the holidays - the blue distance traversed by the railway being in the nature of an ocean between continents.

ELM PARK HOUSE

View of Elm Park School c.1922 from the north. Note the cricket pavilion on the left of the picture.

THE ESTATE AND ITS HISTORY

THE HOUSE AND DEMESNE OF ELM PARK lie just north of the village of Killylea, some five miles west of the city of Armagh. The Ordnance Survey designates the whole townland containing 198 acres as 'Elm Park or Mullaghatinny'. Before the second half of the eighteenth century the townland was known only as Mullaghatinny. It appeared first as 'Mullagh-Itynne' among the townlands recorded at an Inquisition in 1608 into the lands of County Armagh. The original form may have been 'Mullach an tSionaigh' meaning the 'hilltop of the fox'. A small stream forms its eastern boundary with the townland of Tonnagh. To the north is Knappagh which contains another large country house and its parkland, and to the west is Knockaneagh. The southern boundary was redefined in the 1850s by the Armagh to Monaghan railway line.

During the Plantation project in the early seventeenth century the Maxwell family was established at Mullaghatinny and succeeded by their descendants, the Close and Blacker families, who continued to live there until the early twentieth century. The first Maxwell representative was the Rev. Robert Maxwell who crossed to Ireland at the bidding of King James VI 'to secure an interest for him in this kingdom'. In 1610 Maxwell was promoted Dean of Armagh. Although he had no great country estate but resided in a 'poore house in Ardmagh opposite the land of the deanery', he held several other lucrative positions in the church. By the time of his death about 1622, however, he had used his acquired wealth to become a substantial landowner. He had five children; three sons and two daughters. As Dean, he had considerable influence in the church and his strength of will was liable to bring him into conflict with his superiors. It has been suggested that he ruined his chances of further promotion when he prevented Primate Henry Usher from 'making a fee farm grant of the see lands of Armagh at £1500 per year for ever to a dependent of the duke of Buckingham'.

Robert's eldest son, also named Robert, followed his father into the church. He studied at Trinity College Dublin obtaining the degree of Doctor of Divinity and became a Fellow of the College. In 1617 he was ordained and later became chaplain to the Lord Lieutenant. In 1625 he became Prebendary of Tynan, a post he held for a further thirty years. In the same year he married Margaret, daughter of Henry Echlin, Bishop of Down. He was appointed Bishop of Kilmore in 1643.

The destruction of his house in the 1641 rebellion with the murder there of his brother, Lieutenant James Maxwell, and his wife, forced Robert to flee to Dublin from where he was sent to England as a commissioner from the clergy of the Church of Ireland to the King. He remained there until the restoration of King Charles II in 1660, returning only briefly to Dublin in 1643 to be created Bishop of Kilmore. On his return Bishop Robert rebuilt his home at College Hall while his son James built a new house for himself nearby and named it Fellows Hall: both are listed in the Hearth Money Rolls of 1664. The rolls contain no mention, however, of a house at Mullaghatinny that had belonged to the family. Local historian T.G.F. Paterson maintained that Mullaghatinny had been destroyed in the Civil War and not rebuilt until later in the century. It was occupied then by James and Henry Maxwell, two sons of the murdered Lieutenant James. The inhabitants of this property until the beginning of the twentieth century were descended from one of these two boys, Henry Maxwell. He leased the townland from his own relations, the Maxwells of College Hall, and not directly from the Primate. His descendants formed a cadet or junior branch of the Maxwell family and so were not considered as important as the descendants of his uncle, Bishop Robert.

Mullaghatinny was not College land but belonged to the Church and from as early as 1631 Robert Maxwell had leased it with several other townlands from the Primate. In the See of Armagh Rentals for 1631 Connor O'Donellan was recorded as having held property in the territory of Clonall that was now held by Robert Maxwell, clerk. Just to the north of Mullaghatinny, Knappagh had been held by the O'Carra or Corr family or 'the Sept of Moyntercar' as they are called in an inquisition of 1609: this family had held the property 'time out of mind' and paid thirteen shillings and four pence rent to the Primate. Half a century later a See Rental of 1676 records that Bishop Robert Maxwell was then dead and his widow was tenant of the lands in Armagh parish that included 'Mullaghaghterie als Mullaghaghtelee als Mullaghaghteny in the precinct of Clonaule in the county Armagh'. The term 'als' is an abbreviation for 'alias' meaning 'otherwise known as' and its inclusion illustrates the fluidity in the way placenames were recorded and remembered at this time.

By the time of his death in 1672 Bishop Robert had managed to acquire not only substantial property in County Armagh including Fellows Hall and College Hall townlands but also estates at Farnham in County Cavan, and Falkland in County Monaghan. Most of his Armagh estate of over 23,000 acres was leased from Trinity College Dublin. As part of the Plantation scheme the College had been granted many townlands in the western part of County Armagh and the names given by the Maxwells to their houses are a reminder of the identity of their owner. Robert had been a Fellow of the College and may have used his position to acquire College land. He was accused with James Hamilton and the then Provost of the College, Sir William Temple, of shady dealings involving College leases at this time.

Henry stayed at Mullaghatinny and married his cousin Margaret, Bishop

Robert's daughter. Of their three children, the only son James died leaving no male successor and so the two daughters became co-heirs to Mullaghatinny. The elder girl, Phoebe, married a James Gallaspie but there is little information about this union. The younger daughter, Margaret, married Sir Robert Maxwell of Orchardstown in Scotland through whom we can continue to trace the family connection with the house. There were no children from this marriage and after her husband's death she married Captain James Butler of Bramblestown County Kilkenny. Margaret was regarded among the Maxwells as a lady of some standing and was always addressed as 'Dame Margaret' or 'Lady Margaret' Maxwell.

Captain James and Dame Margaret lived at Mullaghatinny and made many improvements to the family residence and its surroundings. In 1703 'A view or an account of the lands of the Archbishop of Armagh' prepared by Thomas Ashe, described the house at Mullaghatinny as a 'very good stone house' of two storeys consisting of handsome rooms, parlour, kitchen and common hall. It confirmed that Butler was leasing the property from Henry Maxwell, who in turn leased from the Primate. Most of the townland of 125 acres Irish Plantation Measure [equivalent to 190 statute acres] grazed cattle or grew corn. The 'great turf bog' was a valuable asset and there was a small wood of alder trees. The Butlers had planted hedges of holly and were encouraging a thriving nursery of Scotch firs: in view of the subsequent name of the property it is surprising that no mention was made of elm trees. Several acres of orchards were 'the best I have seen' according to Ashe. On the stream that flows along the eastern edge of Mullaghatinny, Butler had erected a corn mill. This description of an improving farm and demesne is completed with an account of the farm buildings including a barn, a cow house and 'a new ox house built with stone' as oxen then were still used as draught animals for ploughing.

On the death of the Primate's chief tenant, Henry Maxwell, about 1709 he was succeeded by his son John. In 1756 John was created Baron Farnham and it is from him that the present Lord Farnham is descended.

Dame Margaret and Captain Butler had only one child, a daughter christened Catherine. After Captain Butler's death the Mullaghatinny property was supervised by the ageing Dame Margaret. In 1721 her daughter Catherine married the Rev. Samuel Close (1683-1742) Rector of Donaghenry in County Tyrone and when their son was born in 1722 he was given the Christian name Maxwell to emphasise the connection with that family. Catherine also had four daughters. They included Elizabeth who in 1763 married Peter Gervais, a revenue collector in Armagh, while Margaret married Charles Woolley.

If Dame Margaret and her daughter's family, the Closes, ever lived together at Elm Park during the early part of the century, they seem to have moved elsewhere by 1754. In that year Catherine's son, Maxwell Close, advertised the house for letting with 137 acres of the surrounding townland. The advertisement provides a brief but relevant comment on the scale of the house and farm buildings fifty years after Ashe's 'View'. It was evidently a large and prosperous

THE ESTATE AND ITS HISTORY

> TO be let for such Term as shall be agreed on, from the first Day of May next, the House of Mullatinny, with convenient Offices inclosed with a Wall, viz. a Brew House, with a large Boiler fixed in it, Stabling for twenty Horses, a Turf House that will hold 800 Gage Kishes of Turf, a Cow House that will hold 16 Cows, and a good Barn, all in good Repair; now held by Capt. Maxwell, with a Kitchen Garden and Orchard, and any Number of Acres of Land not exceeding one hundred, thirty-seven of which is Meadow, with sufficient Fireing within a Quarter of a Mile of the House. Mulatinny is but three Miles from Armagh, three of Middletown, and four of Glaslough, all Market Towns.——The House and Land will be shewn by Hugh Mc. Gourk at Mullatinny, and Proposals to be made to Maxwell Close, Esq; at Newtownlemavady in the County Londonderry, or Mr. Gillespy, Merchant in Armagh.

Belfast News Letter, 26 Feb. 1754 advertising the house at Mullaghatinny to let.

farm with stables for twenty horses, a cow house for sixteen cows, a large turf house, a barn, brew house, orchard and a kitchen garden that may well be the enclosed garden today. The residence was still known as 'the house of Mullatinny' and the name Elm Park was not mentioned.

When he was about thirty years old Maxwell Close had moved from County Armagh and taken up residence in Limavady, County Londonderry. It was to him at his northern seat that any offers for the house were to be sent. Where his family lived at this period is not known. His father had died in 1742, and his mother may also have been dead by this time but his grandmother, Dame Margaret, lived until 1758. She bequeathed the property to Maxwell, though he apparently had an influential stake in it prior to this. In 1748 Maxwell Close had married his cousin Mary, daughter of Robert Maxwell of Fellows Hall. He was domiciled in Limavady from at least 1754 and perhaps from his marriage six years earlier. By July 1763, however, he was back in County Armagh and from his uninterrupted involvement after that year in a variety of Armagh institutions, it is probably accurate to conclude that he spent the rest of his days at Elm Park.

When his sister Elizabeth married Peter Gervais on 24 March 1763, it was announced the wedding had taken place 'at Elm Park in the county of Armagh'. Elizabeth or Peter may have renamed the place as they seem to have been living there then. Although the name was applied at first only to the house, within forty years the surrounding lands were also generally known as Elm Park and the original placename was falling into disuse. By 1803 Sir Charles Coote described it simply as the 'demesne of Elm Park'. The transformation of Mullaghatinny that echoed back to the Gaelic past, to fashionable Elm Park reflects the growing confidence of the establishment. Today the townland's proper name is

'Mullaghatinny or Elm Park' but even as early as 1817 it had acquired this double name. This practice of linking Gaelic and English placenames with the word 'or' was adopted by the Ordnance Survey mapmakers in the 1830s in mid-Armagh, notably at Bondville or Tullybrick Etra, Ballynameta or Woodpark, College Hall or Marrassit, Crearum or Fellows Hall, and Fairview or Mucklagh.

As one of the larger country houses in the area Elm Park became a fashionable venue for visits from the local landed gentry. At the end of the century Alexander Hamilton, the son of the Dean of Armagh, recorded in his diary calling at the house several times: 'I rode to pay a visit at the deanery. As I was returning met the Misses Browne and Bess Gervaise riding. I told them I was going to dine at Elm Park, they turned about and went with Bess Close who joined us and we rode till we got near to Elm Park. We went thither to dine and they returned to Armagh. After dinner Jemmy Dawson and I rode into Monaghan. Lightning was playing through the sky before us the whole way'.

Samuel Close (1749-1817) was the eldest son of Maxwell and Mary and, like his grandfather of the same name, he joined the church. He was Rector of Keady from 1780 to 1813 and in that year was appointed Prebendary of Tynan. He married a daughter of the Dean of Clonmacnoise, Deborah Champagne, in 1782. They lived at Elm Park for many years and it was there that they ended their days. When Samuel died of typhus in September 1817, his wife had already been dead two years. During his lifetime Rev. Samuel Close had acquired much property including a parcel of College lands nearby known as the Brootally estate of about 3,000 acres, left to him by his grandfather, Robert Maxwell. By 1803, according to Sir Charles Coote, the Closes had bought out their landlord and possessed Elm Park in freehold. Apart from the estates of Lords Charlemont and Cremorne the Elm Park estate was the only one in the Barony of Armagh held in freehold. The confidence that came with acquiring Elm Park in freehold may have prompted the building project in 1803 when the house was completely remodelled. During the compilation of his *Statistical Survey of the County of Armagh* (1804) Sir Charles Coote commented on the old Elm Park house as 'low and beautifully surrounded by plantations' but he made no mention of its structure.

In his will, Samuel left Elm Park to his eldest son, Colonel Maxwell Close (1783-1867). In 1818 Maxwell, however, bought another County Armagh estate from the Moores of Drumbanagher near Poyntzpass. Ten years later he began replacing the Drumbanagher house with a magnificent mansion designed by the celebrated Scottish architect, William Playfair. That Colonel Close continued to live at Elm Park during this period is confirmed by a local doctor's casebook. Dr William Lodge Kidd meticulously recorded his visits to patients in the Armagh area from 1818 to 1851. An unspecified but chronic illness suffered by Maxwell Close's wife, Anna Brownlow (sister of the first Lord Lurgan), necessitated regular visits from Dr Kidd, thus providing a record of the movements of the family over the years. Until at least May 1831, Maxwell Close and his family

THE ESTATE AND ITS HISTORY

Drumbanagher House near Poyntzpass built by Col. Maxwell Close in the 1830s.

were living at Elm Park but by 12 October that year they had begun to settle into the still unfinished mansion at Drumbanagher. There are hints that other members of the Brownlow family lodged with them both at Elm Park and Drumbanagher. After October 1831 Dr Kidd visited his patients at Drumbanagher rather than at Elm Park.

It is through Maxwell's cousin, Rev. Samuel Blacker (1771-1849), that the story of the family's connection with Elm Park continued. He was the elder son of Samuel's sister, Grace (1750-98), who married in 1767 the Rev. St.John Blacker, the twenty-four year old Rector of Moira and grandson of William Blacker of Carrickblacker, a veteran of the Boyne. Two of their boys, Maxwell and Samuel, were favourite nephews of the Rev. Samuel and inherited all his silver and plate. Samuel entered the church and eventually become Rector of Mullabrack. It is unlikely that he himself ever lived at Elm Park although he was Rector of Tynan from 1817-26. In the latter year he was appointed Rector of Mullabrack parish where he built an opulent glebe house. His eldest son, St.John Thomas Blacker was born in 1822, one of five children. He was the next family member to reside at Elm Park but not until the 1850s. Between the Close family's migration to Drumbanagher in 1831 and St.John Thomas Blacker's residence at Elm Park in the 1850s, the house was occupied by a succession of tenants.

In 1838 the first Townland Valuation by the government found that three-quarters of the demesne at Elm Park was good fertile land that deteriorated in quality towards the south. In the southwest corner of the townland there were about seven acres of boggy land, the remnant of the 'great turf bog' of 1703. A

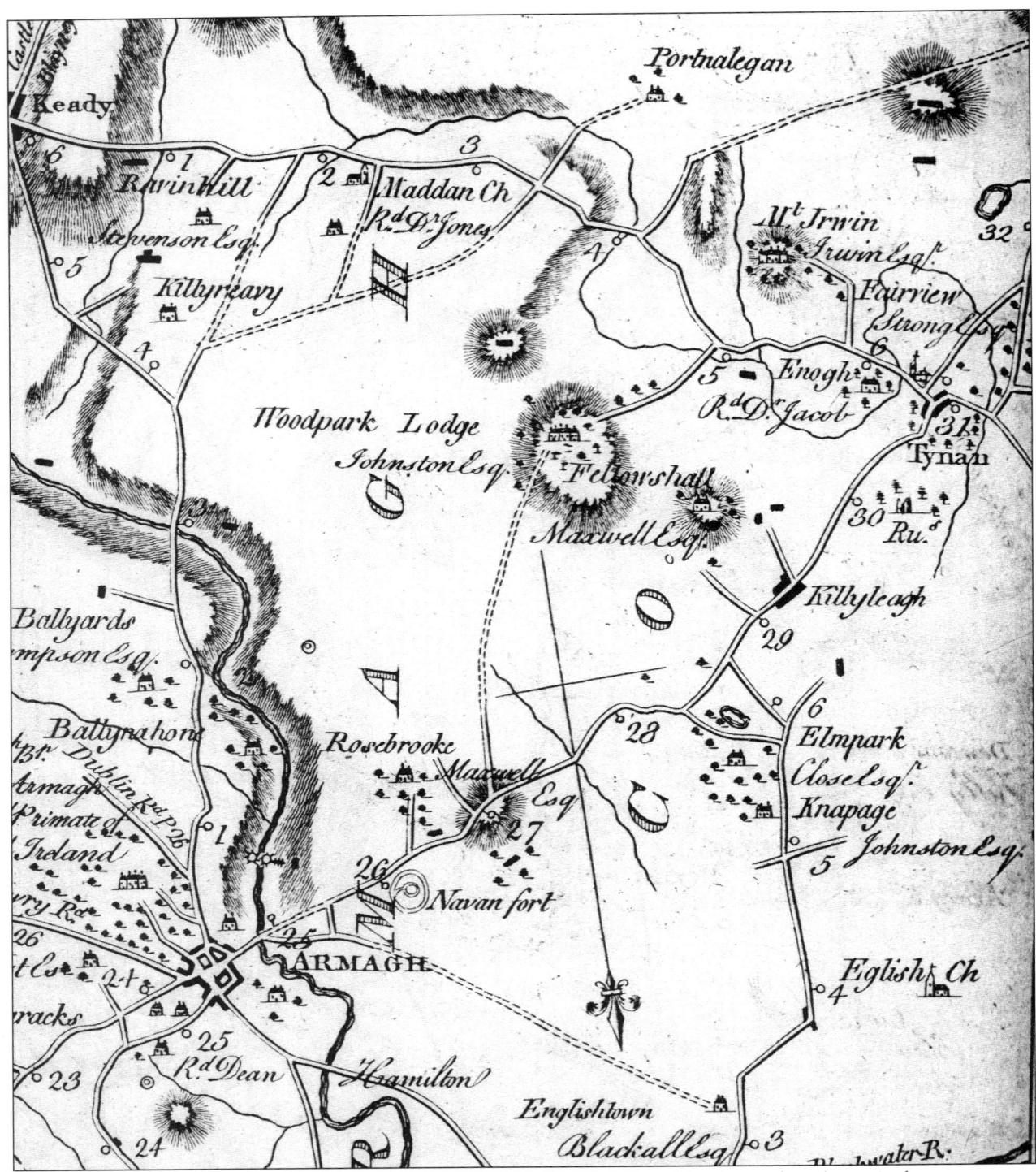

Taylor and Skinner map dating from 1777 shows Elm Park House together with other gentlemen's seats in the area.

THE ESTATE AND ITS HISTORY

little to the east of this was an area close to the stream that separated Mullaghatinny from Tonnagh where the 'wet retentive subsoil' may have been the vestiges of a lake shown on Taylor and Skinner's map of 1777. The first Ordnance Survey map dated 1835 (see frontispiece) illustrates the extent of the plantations with features such as 'rustic bridges' spanning the little stream. The outbuildings are depicted as an enclosed stable block and yard. Two gatelodges stood then at the entrances to the estate. The 1908 map indicates two new lodges that had been built sometime after 1864: one was on the Knappagh road to the north of Elm Park and the other close to Killylea railway station, taking advantage of that new mode of transport. These later gatelodges are much further from the house than the earlier two. As gatelodges mark the boundary between county road and private avenue, their relocation implies expansion of the demesne during the late nineteenth century.

The first tenant in the 1830s was Thomas Knox Armstrong who had previously leased the old Maxwell house, Fellows Hall. He is buried in Rome where a tombstone in the Protestant cemetery records: 'Sacred to the memory of Thomas Knox Armstrong esqre Late of Elm Park in the county of Armagh Ireland Who died in this city on the 13th day of January A.D. 1840 In the 42 year of his age'. He lies in the same cemetery as Keats and only five rows away

Grace Hall near Dollingstown. When St.John Blacker acquired this Douglas property in 1880 he added Douglas to his surname.

Maxwell Vandeleur Blacker-Douglas 1859–1929. *Reproduced with the permission of the Armagh County Museum/MAGNI.*

from Percy Bysshe Shelley. After Armstrong the second Earl of Charlemont lived in the house until 1845 while his county Tyrone residence, Roxborough House at Moy, was being transformed by the architect William Murray.

By 1851 St.John Thomas Blacker had returned to his ancestral home at Elm Park but it was not a convenient place from which to manage several estates throughout Ireland. The Tullahennel estate in County Kerry containing more than 20,000 acres occupied much of his energy: by the end of the century he had spent £40,000 on it. In 1859 his son Maxwell Vandeleur Blacker was born. For much of the 1860s his family resided at Trimblestown Cottage in County Dublin. His interest in Elm Park was undiminished for it is recorded that while living in County Dublin he held Elm Park in freehold. By 1870 the family had returned north and was residing at Elm Park once more. In 1880 he assumed the

St. John Blacker-Douglas 1822–1900. *Reproduced with the permission of the Armagh County Museum/MAGNI.*

additional surname of Douglas on inheriting the estate of his uncle at Grace Hall near Dollingstown in County Down.

Shortly after inheriting the Grace Hall estate, St.John embarked on major improvements to Elm Park. Blacker-Douglas's agent boasted later that £20,000 had been spent on it including modern farm buildings. Although it is not clear how extensively the outbuildings were altered or rebuilt, the fact that a datestone bearing the date 1884 is set over the entrance to the yard indicates that at least some of the fine stone out-offices nearby were built at this time. However, the most noticeable changes resulting from this phase of improvement was on the south side of the house where a new block was constructed and the elaborate conservatory added. The conservatory and sunny garden terrace feature in many photographs of the house. The dining room behind the conservatory with its

Lieut Robert Blacker-Douglas 1892–1915. *Reproduced with the permission of the Armagh County Museum/MAGNI.*

elaborately moulded plasterwork ceiling was also added at this time, as was the block immediately to the east with its balcony. The architect responsible for this work was James Rawson Carroll of Dublin: a carefully executed ink wash drawing of the new phase is in the collection of Armagh County Museum.

Although Elm Park was certainly important to St.John Blacker-Douglas he concentrated more of his attention on the other properties he owned throughout Ireland. St.John served as High Sheriff for Armagh in 1861 and in Kerry in 1865. His son, Maxwell Vandeleur Blacker-Douglas, was also appointed High Sheriff of County Kerry and later of County Dublin. Although Elm Park was described as one of his seats, it was by the turn of the century home only to his widowed mother. His residence from at least 1904 to 1916 was at 2 Bellvue Park, Killiney, County Dublin.

THE ESTATE AND ITS HISTORY

The elaborate memorial dedicated to several generations of the Blacker family in Killylea parish church. *Photograph courtesy Alan Ellison.*

St. John Blacker-Douglas died 26 September 1900. Just over six months later the 1901 census recorded details of the Elm Park household and estate and concluded that it was still very much a grand house with all the usual facilities expected in such a residence. There were six stables with three coach houses and a harness room, and ten cow houses with calf houses and a diary. There was a barn, piggery, and fowl house as well as a potato store, a workshop and a laundry. Inside the house there were forty rooms and ten people lived there. The sixty-seven year old widow, Mrs Elizabeth Blacker-Douglas, enjoyed presiding over such splendid surroundings. Jenny Porter was the cook and Mary Lynch the housekeeper. The lady's maid and housemaid were Elisa Whelan and Fanny Greer while Ellen Hepenstall and Agnes Clark worked as maids. The three male staff were John Banchall, the butler, Robert Cogrell the page and Robert McCall

ELM PARK: COUNTRY HOUSE TO PREPARATORY SCHOOL

HOUSES, ETC, TO BE LET OR SOLD.

TO BE SOLD,

ELM PARK,

KILLYLEA, COUNTY ARMAGH,

The Property of MAXWELL V. BLACKER DOUGLAS, D.L., Bellevue, Killiney, County Dublin,

WITH 270 ACRES OF LAND OR LESS.

THE HOUSE, WHICH IS IN EXCELLENT CONDITION, contains Large Entrance Hall, four Reception-rooms, Billiard-room, Conservatory, 14 Bed and Dressing Rooms, two Bathrooms, Domestic Offices, Servants' Rooms; Motor Garage, Stabling (Musgrave's) for eight horses.

Three Lodges, Steward's House, two Cottages, well laid-out Pleasure Grounds, Tennis and Croquet Lawns; well-stocked, walled-in Fruit and Vegetable Garden with Greenhouses, &c.

The Park is well timbered and contains 270 acres of the best arable and grazing lands in Ulster, which, having been farmed by the owner, are in the best state of cultivation. Five acres of good Orchard planted 7 years.

The Farm Buildings are commodious and up to date.

Elm Park is situated half a mile from Killylea Station, G.N. Rly. (one Gate Lodge being at the station), 40 by road from Belfast, and 4 miles from Armagh.

Hounds—Tynan and Armagh Hunt. Within easy reach of County Down Stag Hounds.

Golf Links, Tennis and Cricket Clubs—Armagh.

For further particulars, apply to

MAJOR J. C. BOYLE,

Estate Office, Armagh.

Advertisement in the Belfast News Letter *for the sale of Elm Park in the autumn of 1919.*

the groom. The outdoor staff, some of whom stayed on when the house was sold and the school opened, are not included, but they lived nearby. John Campbell was the gardener and Thomas Kerr was described as a garden labourer. While Campbell lived alone, Kerr lived with his wife and three young children. Another garden labourer, William McParlan, lived with his wife and family of two in another of the four modest houses around the demesne. William's twenty-four year old son, John, also worked in the Elm Park gardens. The other family living in the demesne was the Linton family, a name that features often throughout the life of the school. John Linton was the Jack-of-all-trades who kept the place in good order and would have been called on to do any number of odd jobs. His occupation on the census form is carpenter and it may have been him or his son John who took woodwork classes in the prep school during the 1920s and 1930s.

By the outbreak of the First World War most of the townland of Elm Park was being let and farmed to generate cash. The estate was liable to an increasing rate of income tax. For instance, in the year 1915-16 tax was assessed at £87 but by 1917-18 this figure had risen to £148 and by the year 1918-19 the first instalment was £130. The First World War had also depleted the male labour force and wages offered to potential staff at Elm Park were simply being declined. Although old Mrs Blacker-Douglas lived at Elm Park with her retinue of servants until her death aged eighty-five in 1919 it was her son Maxwell Blacker-Douglas who dealt with the running of the estate. The estate may have been intended for Maxwell Blacker-Douglas's son, Robert, but his death in February 1915 while serving as Lieutenant with the Irish Guards in France threw the whole future of both the estate and the house as a family seat into confusion. Soon after Maxwell's mother died on 2 September 1919 preparations began for the sale of Elm Park. The stock, crops and farm implements were sold separately early in 1920.

The newspaper advertisements in September attracted an initial rush of interest from speculators. Although several applicants claimed they would farm

A view of the house from the north *c*.1922.

Elm Park, the entrance hall at the time of Mrs Blacker-Douglas's death, 1919.

the estate, Blacker-Douglas's agent, John Charters Boyle suspected that they might break it up to sell off as small farms. One of the speculators had recently purchased an estate nearby at Benburb and had done precisely that. Another approach came from the Belfast firm of nurserymen, Joseph Orr & Sons, but was too brief to determine whether they planned to use Elm Park for a nursery or as a quiet country retreat for the owner. Maxwell Blacker-Douglas and Boyle wanted to sell the place as a residence. Sir Robert Anderson, chairman of Anderson and McAuley Ltd of Belfast and Lord Mayor of the city in 1908, seemed quite keen to acquire the property. Boyle discussed with Blacker-Douglas what selling-price they might ask from Sir Robert: £25,000 was suggested. Although Anderson went so far as to send someone down to Elm Park to look over the place, nothing further transpired. By the beginning of December only two firm offers had been received, one of £7,000 and the other £8,000.

This correspondence between owner and agent contains little detailed information about the condition of Elm Park demesne and the house itself. 'It contains a large entrance hall, four reception rooms, billiard room, school room, conservatory, twenty bedrooms, domestic offices, servants' room, motor garage, stables for eight horses, central heating, good water supply and in good order.'

Elm Park School's sunny garden terrace showing the conservatory.

Elm Park House from the south taken in 1919. *Reproduced with the permission of PRONI.*

ELM PARK: COUNTRY HOUSE TO PREPARATORY SCHOOL

The conservatory that had been added in the 1880s had a special heating system. There was, however, only one bathroom and five or six water-closets. Some modern but unspecified farm buildings had recently been erected at a cost of £1,000. Boyle repeatedly mentioned that the owner's late father (St.John Blacker-Douglas) had spent £12,000 on the improvements made in the 1880s under the supervision of the architect, J. Rawson Carroll.

The first time the two schoolmasters Hugh Eric Seth-Smith and Willoughby Weaving are recorded to be taking an interest in the property is in a letter of 9 October 1920. Boyle wrote to Blacker-Douglas. 'I have heard from the school master at Holywood, Seth-Smith by name' and added 'it would be a good thing to have a school started there.' Boyle liked the idea of converting the property into a school so much that he considered making special financial arrangements to facilitate their circumstances. He contemplated renting the property to Seth-Smith and Willoughby Weaving as they had not the capital to purchase the place outright. He proposed a ten-year lease at £350 a year with an option to purchase for £7,000 at the end of the term. Weaving and Seth-Smith took 61 acres, about a third of the 198 acres comprised in the townland: the remainder had been leased in portions of thirty acres to farmers for a number of years.

It is worth noting when Mr. Seth-Smith died in 1946 he was registered as the sole owner of the property.

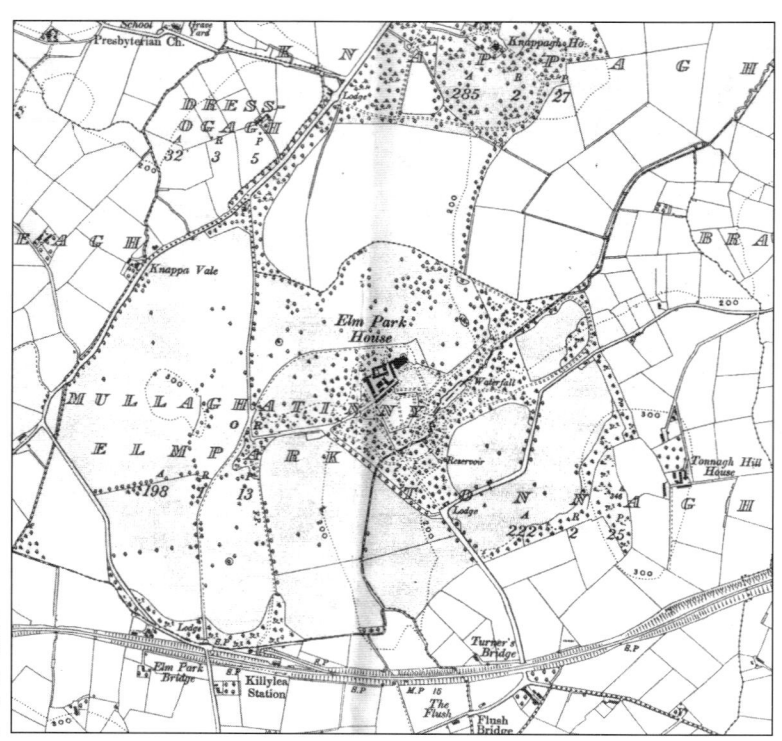

Elm Park House and townland from the 6 inch = 1 mile Ordnance Survey map, 1908 edition.

ELM PARK SCHOOL

Rockport Preparatory School where the two masters taught before founding Elm Park.

THE FOUNDERS

Hugh Eric Seth-Smith and Willoughby Weaving formed a surprising but very effective partnership in their project to establish their own preparatory school in Ulster. They were both graduates from Oxford University but they had studied at different colleges and there is no evidence to suggest they knew each other then. Nor is it known exactly when they came to the north of Ireland. By 1913, however, they were both teaching at Rockport Preparatory School near Craigavad on the County Down coast and living at 31 High Street in Holywood. They both joined the army in 1915 but while Weaving may have been back in Ireland teaching from as early as the beginning of 1916, Seth-Smith was not demobilised until April 1919. He rejoined his old comrade at Rockport. For a while they settled back into the routine of their teaching posts but soon they were actively searching for premises to start their own prep school. There may have been good commercial reasons for starting their own educational establishment. Nevertheless, among those who knew Weaving and Seth-Smith well, there was no doubt that the two men were motivated strongly to educate and inspire the boys in their care. The image of them roaming throughout the counties of Down and Armagh on motorcycle and sidecar during the summer of 1920 searching for a suitable property has become part of Elm Park folklore.

Large country houses provided ideal locations for prep schools. Their isolation ensured minimal interference from the outside world and the countryside was much healthier than a crowded city. Many, such as Rockport and Mourne Grange, both in County Down, had been established near the coast where bracing sea breezes would keep at bay the epidemics of childhood illnesses that so often beset prep schools. For this reason Seth-Smith and Weaving were very interested in Murlough House, the Downshire property in the sandhills near Newcastle. Mr Weaving, however, finally had to admit defeat in a letter to a friend: 'We have done no good about Murlough House … The Downshire agent will not consider the leasing for us as a school. Of course they do not realise that a private school need not make any havoc in a place, and that we could leave it more or less as we found it after a long lease. Anyhow there it is and it is a pity as the place was very suitable and pleasing at the same time'.

Hugh Eric Seth-Smith was born in Westminster on 23 November 1887, the only son of a barrister. His family (known simply as Smith prior to the mid-nineteenth century) owned considerable property in London where it had

THE FOUNDERS

speculated in building developments in the early nineteenth century, notably Wilton Terrace in Belgravia. He was an only son and had two sisters, Grace and Muriel. His mother died when he was three years old and his father four years later. Although Hugh Eric probably grew up at the family home of Silvermere at Cobham in Surrey, little is known of his early life.

The family appears to have been prone to an inherited eye disorder and it has been suggested that Hugh Eric's fear of passing this condition on to another generation was the reason he never married. Certainly some members of the family were blind and Hugh Eric's sister, Muriel, left £2,000 in her will to the Commonwealth Society for the Blind. Hugh Eric himself was treated in 1919 for a corneal ulcer which may have been a symptom of the family weakness.

Hugh Eric was educated at Malvern College and went up to Brasenose College Oxford in the Lent (spring) term of 1907. He was awarded his BA on 8 August 1912 and his MA on 1 May 1919. Although he had a reputation as an all-round sportsman during his time at Elm Park he brought no record of college sporting achievements from Oxford. He joined the army in July 1915 and was soon wounded but returned later to France to serve throughout the war. (For an account of his military career see Appendix 4.)

Although he appeared rather remote and austere, H.E. Seth-Smith had an outgoing and positive approach to life and work. He represented the public face of the school and was always the first point of contact for parents. He believed in Victorian values and was a strict disciplinarian. It comes therefore as something of a surprise to learn that Seth-Smith and

Hugh Eric Seth-Smith 1927, in typical pose with two of his pet dogs.

Weaving were agreed in refusing to use corporal punishment. In its absence discipline was maintained at Elm Park by the imposition of penalty points, or 'conduct marks'. Minor lapses in behaviour were usually dealt with by giving the boy half a conduct mark. At the end of term a special section at the bottom of each school report recorded the number of conduct marks imposed.

Although the boys referred to the headmaster as 'Putty', no one was sure of the origin of the nickname; it seems to have evolved over the years from Sutty or Setty, the schoolboy's adaptation of Seth-Smith. In school photos he is always seen with his pet dogs: Puck was a spaniel and there was a terrier called Fuss. He also owned Clodagh, a labrador, and much later Timoshenko.

Seth-Smith and Weaving both saw themselves as an integral part of that section of society who occupied neighbouring houses such as Tynan Abbey, Fellows Hall and Castle Leslie. In a very real sense they saw themselves, but especially Mr Seth-Smith, as successors to the Blacker-Douglas dynasty. Each year at the end of the summer term the big rooms were cleared of the schoolroom paraphernalia and replaced by household furniture befitting a gentleman's residence. Boys who had occasion to call during the holidays were struck by the transformation of their functional classrooms. Visits during the summer from the Stronge, Armstrong and Leslie families were not uncommon. The Miss McClintocks of Fellows Hall were also frequent guests especially the eldest sister Isa who 'was very friendly with Mr Seth-Smith'. That members of the local landed gentry recognised the value and quality of the educational work at Elm Park is evident from the names of boys from the Stronge and Armstrong families appearing in the school

Willoughby Weaving in 1922.

THE FOUNDERS

Left to right: John Cowdy, Willow and Michael Addeley c.1939.

register. Even during the school terms certain personal reminders of Seth-Smith's background were evident. A large family portrait hung in the dining room and much of the furniture at Elm Park originally had graced the rooms of Silvermere House.

Seth-Smith was a tireless worker and administered not just the school but also Elm Park farm and dairy. He was closely involved in Killylea parish and was a churchwarden from as early as 1924. During the Second World War he took command of Killylea Home Guard and spent much of his time and energy in these roles. These extramural duties were compounded by a sudden, considerable influx of boys more than doubling the school population. Parents' fears of sending their sons across the U-boat infested Irish Sea to prep schools in England made Elm Park an attractive option. To cope with the increased numbers, more staff and space was needed and the school became a larger institution in many ways. All these things increased Seth-Smith's workload and it seems ultimately took a toll on his health. He died suddenly in his sleep on the last day of the winter term of 1946 in his sixtieth year. His passing was a very serious blow to the future of Elm Park School from which it never really recovered.

His colleague, Harry Willoughby Weaving, was born in 1882 and educated near the family home at Abingdon School, Oxford. A few years older than Seth-Smith, he entered Pembroke College Oxford in 1905 and obtained his BA in January 1911 and MA in May 1912. He was said to have achieved a double first in classics and mathematics. In 1913 he published a volume containing eighty-three poems, the first of ten volumes of his poetry: the last appeared thirty-nine years later in 1952. Willow, as he was known to the boys, was a quiet, scholarly soul whose personality neatly complemented that of Seth-Smith. Like Hugh Eric

Seth-Smith, Weaving had joined up to fight in World War One but after less than two months in the trenches was invalided back to Dover with heart trouble. His friend and mentor, poet Robert Bridges, wrote on his behalf to the War Office suggesting that he should work with recruits on this side of the English Channel. He was discharged as unfit for military service. For a full account of his military service see Appendix 4 by Robin Charley.

Willow was a talented and inspiring teacher who left an impression on every boy he taught. His pupils assert that he never lost his temper and never used a cross word to anyone. His mild behaviour should have made discipline a major problem for him. Nevertheless the boys did not take advantage of his kindness and behaved well in his presence. The secret of his success lay in his fertile imagination and his ability to tell stories that kept boys both interested and guessing. He seemed to inspire wonder: one boy described him as 'the man of magic' at Elm Park. At break time a crowd of eager listeners would jostle around him as he regaled them with stories: sixty years later men still recall the scent of wallflowers on the terrace at Elm Park while listening to Willow's stories. Another of his talents, though less often displayed, was playing the flute. One boy whose curiosity led him to enquire from the master the name of the tune that he was playing elicited a cryptic reply that remained vivid in his memory ever after. Willow simply said 'Peacock pudding and pumpkin pie, the great cat scratched the little cat's eye. Hey Jim along Jose oh, The great cat scratched the little cat's tail!'

In the passage of time the literary achievements of Willoughby Weaving have been forgotten. Yet although his published poems may not be well known today, his correspondence with Robert Bridges proves that writing poetry played a major role in his life and that he had earned approval from several well-known names in the literary world. In the introduction to one of his early books of poetry Bridges wrote: 'He sent me some poems a few years ago, while still an under-graduate at Oxford, and ever since that day has had my sympathy and encouragement'. Weaving's many letters to his friend, the Ulster writer Richard Rowley (the pen name of R.V. Williams, father of Michael Williams the last headmaster of Elm Park) express his delight and sometimes frustration at the progress of his latest work. In his book *Heard Melodies* Weaving wrote, 'I cannot let these poems go to press without acknowledging my gratitude to my friend, Mr Richard Rowley, for his many beautiful amendments which, without exception I think, I have used'.

It was not unusual for a member of staff in a prep school to compose poetry or prose. The poet W.H. Auden taught at The Downs, Colwall, while T.S. Eliot was an assistant master at Highgate Junior School and C. Day Lewis taught at the Eton 'nursery', Summer Fields, before moving to Larchfield School in Glasgow. A teaching post at such a school allowed men of literary talent to earn a living while also giving them the freedom and time to pursue their gift. Weaving is virtually unknown in his home town of Abingdon where he spent his final years. It is a pity also that he is not recognised as a poet in County Armagh, where he wrote and found inspiration for over thirty years.

Although not by any means a recluse Mr Weaving's temperament meant that he did not take part much in the wider social life of the district, but confined himself to the school and his own literary work. Just a year before the school closed in 1954, Mr Weaving retired at the age of seventy-one and went to live at 40 Park Road in his home town of Abingdon with his sister whom he survived. During his retirement many of the Elm Park boys kept in touch and some visited him. One of the boys who went to see him at his large terraced house remembers the old man confined to bed but cheerful and delighted to receive visitors. He also recalled seeing buckets on the stairs strategically placed to catch water from the leaky roof. Afterwards some of the boys contributed money and a large fridge was bought for him as a present. Willoughby Weaving died on 16 February 1976 aged 94.

Weaving was the more scholarly of the two men although they both were very capable teachers. Seth-Smith taught French and most other subjects to the level required for the Common Entrance Exam. His down-to-earth teaching style contrasted with the flair of Weaving in teaching English. Weaving was a wonderful raconteur and spellbound the boys with his stories. This persuaded them to read more and he lent books to those who wished to broaden their reading. Weaving also held a special test in mathematics every Friday: anyone who managed to get top marks three weeks running was excused for the following week. He also provided coaching in Latin and Greek for boys entering for scholarships to public schools.

Willow's best-remembered talent was the skilful telling of his legendary dormitory stories which enthralled all those who heard them. This treat was taken from dormitory to dormitory each night and if by chance a boy had misbehaved during the day and earned a conduct mark, the consequences fell on his fellows for the whole dormitory would be 'put off story' that night. The threat of missing an exciting episode was incentive enough to encourage good behaviour. Years later as adults many boys found to their disappointment that Mr Weaving had actually drawn on published books for his exciting tales. Sometimes they were taken from books by Dornford Yates which featured the infamous Dr Grundt (Der Stelser) or Dr Clubfoot who made the sound 'Stump-Stoof' as he walked. These stories were filled with evil Germans and spies and heroes who triumphed in the end. The unanimous groan of 'Oh Sir!' was always the response when Willow announced that the next episode would follow in a week's time.

The Avenue leading to Elm Park House.

INTEGRATION

Prep schools were intended for boys between the ages of seven and fourteen. It was considered beneficial for boys to take them out of their home environment so that they could develop attributes that would stand them in good stead at public school and indeed later in life. Separation also from older boys was considered essential by nineteenth century pioneers who considered that 'public schools are the very seats and nurseries of vice'.

For many boys who attended Elm Park prep school the process of separating them from their families began on the railway platform in Belfast. Mr Seth-Smith would be there, having booked a carriage in which the boys would travel. As the train journeyed through Lisburn, Lurgan, Portadown and Armagh, it picked up more boys on the way. The rail link was an important asset to Elm Park and the proximity of Killylea station to the school gates must have been a positive factor when the two masters discovered the location. Mr Scott who was the Station Master at Killylea railway station with Martin and Kevin Hughes was always a great help at the start and end of terms when the boys' luggage needed to be ferried to and from the school.

The school's unique mode of mechanical transportation met the boys at Killylea. Known as 'the invention' it comprised the chassis of a bullnosed Morris Cowley circa 1921, on which suitable seating and fittings had been expertly attached by its inventor, Mr Bob Mitchell, the individual who played a key role in ensuring the smooth day-to-day running of the school services. He used 'the invention' to pull the trailer into which the boys' trunks and belongings were loaded. The boys themselves walked from the station up the long avenue to the school.

One of the first tasks awaiting them whenever they settled into their new surroundings was to write home to their parents assuring them that they had arrived in one piece. Seth-Smith had had a set of picture postcards of the school printed in the early 1920s and it was on the back of these sepia views of the old Georgian house and grounds that the boys' first brief messages were sent to waiting mothers and fathers. When one boy dutifully sent his card home at the start of a new term in 1940, he wrote merely, 'Arrived safely. Top school captain. I am in Barnet and in Mr Weaving's table'.

At the start of term a new boy could often feel a very small part of a very large institution, isolated as it was in its own extensive grounds. But the fact that he

ELM PARK: COUNTRY HOUSE TO PREPARATORY SCHOOL

was one of many boys in the same situation meant that soon common interests were discovered and new friends made. Most of the boys sent to Elm Park were from upper-middle-class backgrounds and therefore there was a fair chance that they would have known of each other's families. A high proportion of the boys were from families then prominent in the north of Ireland linen industry. (See Appendix 2 prepared by John Cowdy.)

The mention of the dormitory on the postcard introduced the next potential trauma for new boys. Some of them admitted that they were not used to the company of their peers and to face the prospect of sharing a dormitory with strangers was daunting. Like the typical English prep school Elm Park's small dormitories were denominated by historic names, in this case battles fought during the Wars of the Roses. The dorms in Elm Park were called St. Albans, Barnet, Northampton, Tewkesbury, Blore Heath, Towton, Wakefield, Bosworth and Mortimer's Cross.

They reflected the division of the school into two opposing houses for sports day and house matches: White Rose versus Red Rose. But the schoolrooms and dormitories also proved ideal playgrounds. Marbles could be very competitive involving huge gains and losses. If you were skilled at playing 'holies' which utilised the knotholes in the floorboards of the schoolroom then you might come back from a devastating loss made during a game of 'ringies'. The vast terrain of Elm Park's wooden floors was ideal for racing Dinky cars and letters home

One of Elm Park School's spartan dormitories, with high ceilings and shuttered windows.

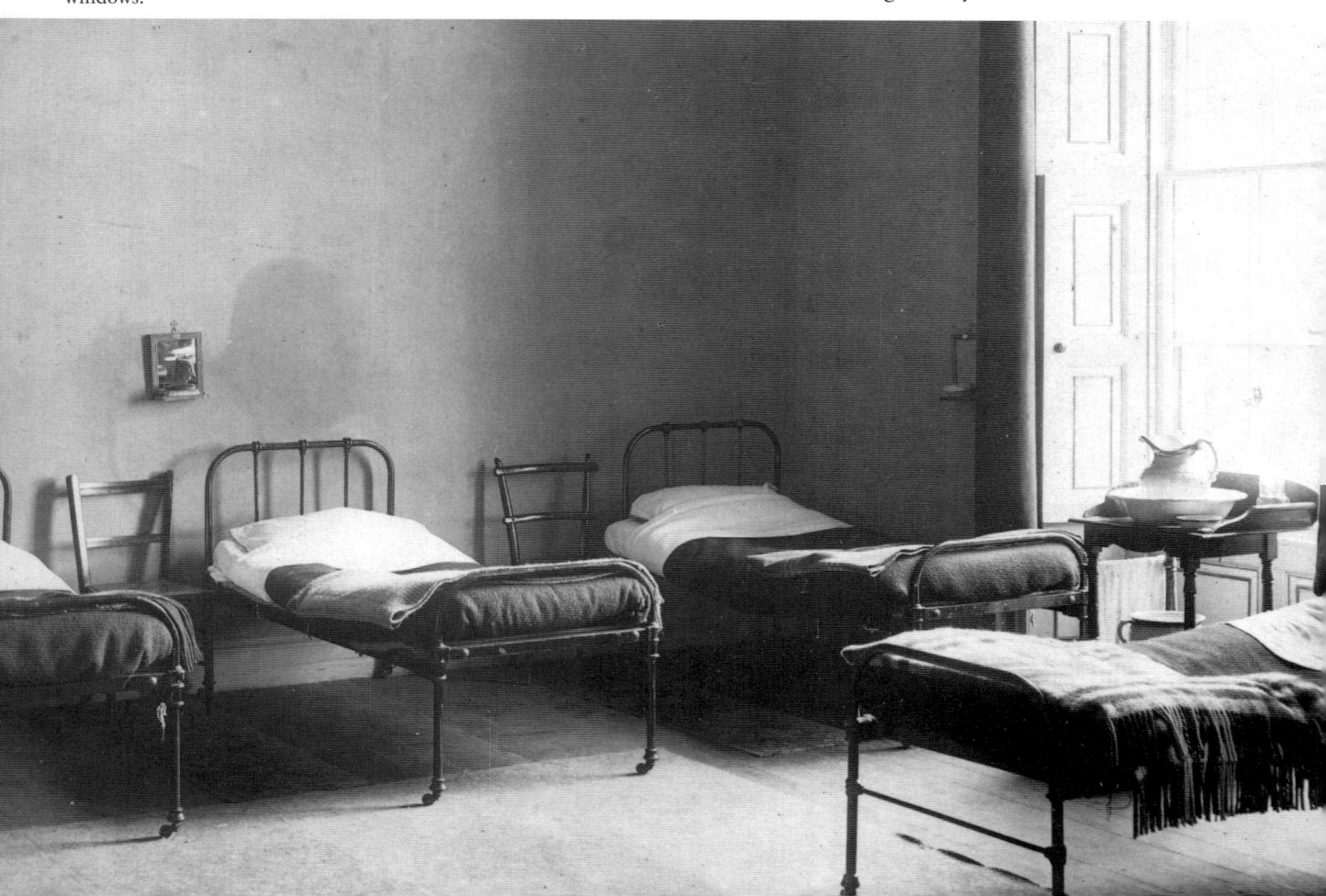

contained urgent requests for the immediate supply of more advanced models to the circuit at Killylea.

Card games were always popular and stakes of treasured collections of cigarette cards could be decimated during an afternoon's pontoon session. The unfortunate bankrupt then had to begin again by purchasing half a card from a friend. Like cigarette cards and marbles, *Beano* and *Dandy* comics were legitimate currency in the school and were freely bartered. One boy's father with the well meant intention of encouraging his son to enjoy reading French, sent him regular copies of a French comic, *L'Herrison* (The Hedgehog). It was declared invalid currency and so its owner 'didn't get to read many comics'.

Many of the boys spent their spare time accumulating stamp collections. The approval system through the post provided the recipient with a batch of assorted stamps from which selections could be made and then paid for. For small boys the expectation of bulging packages of unusual stamps from exotic countries generated great excitement and there was always the prospect of finding a valuable stamp. Both Mr Weaving and Mr Seth-Smith had their own stamp collections and Mr Seth-Smith had a rare Western Australia inverted swan.

The living conditions at Elm Park are summed up quite well by one of the boarders: 'By the decadent and luxurious standards of today, I suppose Elm Park was more like a prison camp than a school in many ways'. No doubt the boys also got up to all sorts of mischief. When some bright spark discovered that the V-shaped bedsprings could be converted into excellent catapults, many uncomfortable nights were spent by boys who sacrificed their sleep for the status acquired from owning state-of-the-art weapons. The rivalry between dorms would frequently lead to inter-dorm wars and raiding parties used the jugs of water from the washstands to dowse their enemy's mattresses before retiring, probably to await a revenge raid.

Strangely no accounts of secret cigarette smoking have yet come to light but many recall a rustic alternative where beech leaves or geranium leaves were rolled in blotting paper and smoked. This practice quickly fell from fashion when rumours began circulating (probably started by staff), that the consequences were appalling stomach ulcers.

For many of the boys this was not only their first time away from home alone but also their first time among children of their own age. Some boys made friends more easily than others and some personalities were bound to clash. Boys who had been over-indulged at home had to learn how to behave themselves in company. As one of them freely admitted, 'I was a difficult delinquent and sometimes uncontrollable boy'. Although by all accounts

Henry Blood-Smyth whose family came from Dublin attended Elm Park from 1938.

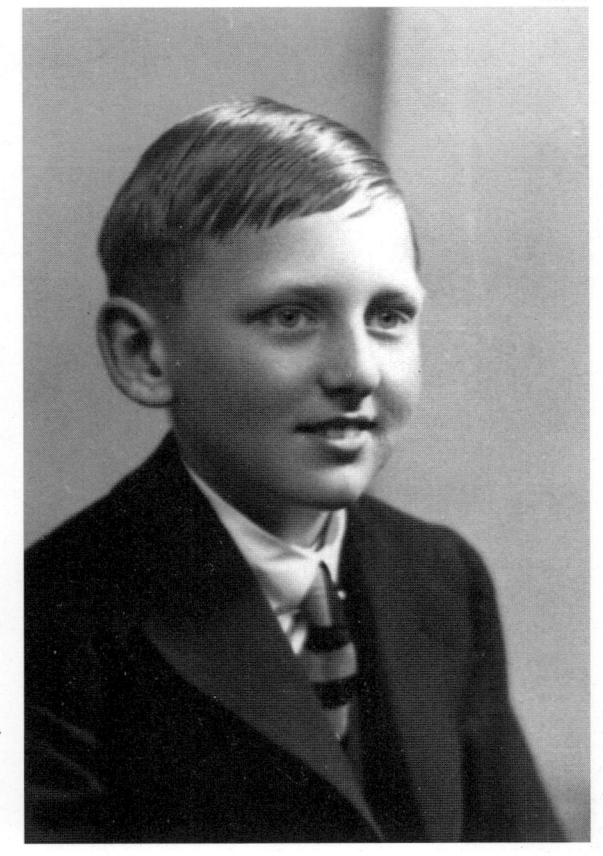

ELM PARK: COUNTRY HOUSE TO PREPARATORY SCHOOL

bullying was not prevalent or endemic at Elm Park, it did occur from time to time. Sensitive boys and those whose character compelled them to react dramatically when provoked, were most likely to attract the attention of bullies. There were occasions when teasing became harassment. Several boys witnessed a first year boy being sent hurtling down into the Glen on a bicycle. The fact that the terrified boy had never learned to ride a bicycle meant this horseplay was actually dangerous bullying. This attack exposed the darker sides of school life and the victim ran away a few days afterwards.

In the early years of the school some of the younger boys are said to have been lowered into the dark interior of the sinister old icehouse in the Glen, a relic from the days when the house was home to the Close and Blacker families. The icehouse was a place of mystery and foreboding and generated its own myths. The threat of being lowered into the dark interior of the icehouse was a chilling one. In the summer of 1948 it was not the juniors but a couple of the female teachers who were threatened with confinement within its dank walls. As a boy boasted in a letter to his parents, 'This afternoon we tried to force Miss Brownell and Miss Shea to go down a pit in the glen called the ice house but she refused and managed to get three slugs on her blouse and there was panic'. In the summer of 1949 some of the boys uncovered the long-buried air vent of the icehouse.

Bobby Boulton (standing)
and Franklin Cardy *c.*1950.

David Strachan's plan of the old icehouse in the Glen.

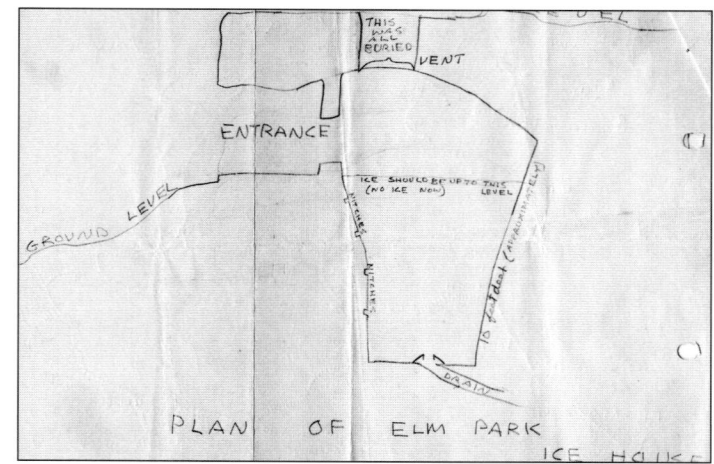

THE SCHOOL DAY

At Elm Park the daily routine was very much part of the whole ethos of preparation. Order and promptness were understood as important values that would serve the boys well in the future. Early timetables and the memories of the boys themselves tell us that the school day began at 7a.m. when pupils were wakened by the first bell. The boys lined up in the conservatory each morning to make their way down to the rather smelly lavatories. When numbers were at their height during the war this essential duty was accomplished with efficient military precision: there were wooden batons or tokens which were passed relay fashion whilst coming and going from the WCs, therefore ensuring a 'proper' number used the lavatories at any one time.

After preparing their beds for the maid who would come later to make them, each boy stood alongside his and waited for Putty to cast a critical eye in his direction. He asked, 'Have you washed your teeth?' and received the reply 'Yes Sir'. When the headmaster's inspection was complete, everyone went to breakfast. After breakfast and prayers, classes began at 9 o'clock. There were four classes in the morning with a twenty-minute break and then lunch at about 1p.m.

SCHEME OF WORK.

7.45 a.m.—8.0 a.m.	Prayers.
8.0 a.m.—8.30 a.m.	Breakfast
9.0 a.m.—1.0 p.m.	Lessons; four periods of 50 minutes each, with intervals of 10 minutes. Light Lunch at 10.50.
1.15 p.m.	Dinner.
2.30 p.m.—4.0 p.m.	Games. At 4 o'clock the Boys have biscuits.
4.30 p.m.—6.0 p.m.	Lessons; two periods of 45 minutes.
6.0 p.m.—6.30 p.m.	Tea.
6.30 p.m.—7.30 p.m.	Preparation.
7.0 p.m.	The smaller Boys go to bed.
7.30 p.m.	Prayers.
7.30 p.m.—8.30 p.m.	Reading. Boys are encouraged to read to themselves for this period.
8.30 p.m.	Bedtime.
9.0 p.m.	Lights Out.

¶ There are half-holidays on Wednesdays and Saturdays, and on Saturday evenings there is no preparation.

A typical school timetable from the 1920s.

The schoolroom *c.* 1922.

At the morning break the boys played all sorts of games on a triangular patch of ground that they referred to as Tri-Nac or Trinac (after Trinacia, the classical poetic term for the triangular island of Sicily which this patch of ground resembled in shape). Someone, for example, would shout 'last touch the tree for Charlie' which grew near the centre of Trinac. The first boy who managed to escape from the classrooms ran to the centre of Trinac and on touching the tree became Charlie. The game, sometimes called 'Charlie over the water', was a rough and ready variation of tig when Charlie would try to tig any of the other boys as they raced past him. Once caught they joined forces with their captor to catch the others but they were handicapped by having to hold hands in a chain.

One of the boys working in the schoolroom *c.*1950.

As their numbers mounted the potential for collisions and accidents increased but that was all part of the rough and tumble of the game.

After lunch there was another period of play, usually games like cowboys and Indians, before the afternoon hockey, football or cricket match that commenced about 2.30p.m. During a short break about 4.30p.m. milk and biscuits were provided in the large conservatory full of potted geraniums and tall climbing plants like mimosa. It contained a tank of goldfish and at one time a small aviary of budgerigars.

Another two classes followed the afternoon break until tea about 6.30p.m. Prep followed until 7.30p.m. when the smaller boys went to bed. The older ones were encouraged to spend some time reading quietly until 8.30p.m. when they followed. By 9 o'clock all the dormitory lights were out. Under the bedclothes, however, torches provided light for reading and headphones access to the programmes such as 'Appointment with Fear', broadcast on the novel crystal radio sets.

The goal post in 'Trinac' Summer 1949.

The conservatory as it was in the 1920s. Mr Seth-Smith maintained it at a high standard. Mimosas, passionflowers and climbing geraniums flourished here. At one time there was also a fish-tank and a small aviary in the conservatory.

COMINGS AND GOINGS

ANOTHER ASPECT OF THE SEPARATION PHILOSOPHY exercised at Elm Park concerned parental visits. Mr Seth-Smith and Mr Weaving saw in themselves a pair of dedicated guardians with the vocation and talent to care for the boys in their charge. During term-time parents were required to abide by this arrangement. For parents to drop in unannounced was viewed as a disruptive influence and it probably would have been, particularly for boys in their first term. The process of adjusting to the new environment could all too easily be disturbed by too many reminders of home. This philosophy extended to home visits as well: there were no half-term breaks at Elm Park. As well as the perceived benefits of entrusting the boy to the care of the school for the whole term, another reason for this may have been the fear of bringing back germs to the enclosed environment of the school.

Parental visits were restricted to Saturday afternoons from 2 to 5p.m. and visiting parents were not permitted to take their children out of the school grounds. Again, the masters may have had good reason for enforcing the latter

A group of boys dressed for the walk to church on a Sunday morning. Left to right: Gerry Fitzgibbon, V. Whyte, Norman Ferguson, C. Proctor, A. Fforde, Adrian Forest, John Pringle, Desmond Titterington and R. Turner.

rule. Many of the boys lived at such a distance from the school that frequent visits from their mother and father would have been inconvenient. It would be unfair to them if one of their friends were to be whisked away on regular sprees beyond the confines of the grounds. Usually their only official excursion out of their academic asylum was the long walk to church on Sundays or away matches to other schools.

Sunday morning was dominated by the walk to church which could be a kind of adventure in itself and some saw it as a major expedition. The usual place of worship was Killylea Church of Ireland a few miles away but there were occasions when the long crocodile of boys turned around and instead walked north to Drumsallen Church on the hill above Knappagh. During the summer term on hot Sunday mornings many boys could be seen busily making preparations for this journey. Empty inkbottles were rinsed out and filled with water and lemonade powder to sustain the walkers. The ever present fear of contagious diseases sometimes led to the Sunday morning being spent in other ways. Writing home in the spring of 1948 David Strachan said 'We did not go to church this morning because there is a disease in Killylea but we went for a walk instead'. On another occasion the boys who owned bicycles rode them to church

David Strachan who attended Elm Park 1946-50.

ELM PARK: COUNTRY HOUSE TO PREPARATORY SCHOOL

A group of boys dressed for church on Sunday morning.

Five boys standing on the stump of the beech tree that was felled in the autumn of 1950. Left to right: Michael Acheson, Corry Caruth, [?] Gordon, Ricky Blundel, Colin Stoupe.

in Benburb and sometimes in the summer the older cyclists would go into Armagh to the cathedral. A letter from Mr Weaving records one such expedition, 'The cyclists are going to Derrynoose to church to-morrow and Mrs Campbell has kindly asked them to lunch'. Mrs Campbell was the wife of the Rector and their son, Morris Campbell, was a pupil at Elm Park.

The main attraction at Drumsallen Church was the fat boy who manually pumped the organ. It was always a temptation for the Elm Park boys to pull faces at him so that his rhythmic pumping would flounder. Churchgoing may not have brought such distractions for all. Several boys subsequently joined the ranks of the clergy and one of the young masters who taught there in the Thirties, Mr Owen, later became Bishop of Limerick.

Back at school after church there were two other tasks to be performed before release came for an afternoon of high adventure. The collect of the day had to be learned off by heart and then a letter was written home, usually a plea for whatever was the latest craze.

Left to right: Drew Henderson, Norman Ferguson, Alan Knighton Smith, Michael Mackie, John Kinnaird and Jim Pringle, *c.*1941.

A large degree of freedom was enjoyed by the boys and although there were unwritten rules as to the extent of their wanderings, Elm Park demesne afforded them a rural playground that few places could match. The woods beside the house were full of mature timber but closer to the house an ancient beech tree stood like a monument to the landscaping efforts of the previous occupants. It was showing signs of decay and so when a large branch fell onto the tennis court during the summer holidays of 1950, it was decided essential to remove the dangerous tree altogether. For many boys the contest between the workmen and the old tree on 18 October has remained one of their most enduring memories of Elm Park. One boy wrote home dramatically describing the process blow by blow: 'Finally at 6.50 they tried again, and the poor tree came down with a terrible crash and crackling of broken branches, the ground shook like an earthquake, one of the men was nearly killed because a root shot up underneath his feet and he only just got off in time … the place certainly looks very bare without it. I have drawn you a plan showing exactly what happened'. The *coup de grace* was recalled by one boy who watched when the stump was blown up with gelignite.

Although there was plenty of space to enjoy around the school, some boys roamed further than others and a dare or bet to run as far as the demesne wall of Knappagh and back was considered an excursion into alien territory. Nearby orchards were raided too at the appropriate time of year. Of course the railway line from Armagh to Monaghan was always an attractive proposition. Pennies were left on the line and the boys retired to wait for them to be flattened by a passing train.

ELM PARK: COUNTRY HOUSE TO PREPARATORY SCHOOL

Left to right: Robert Twigg, Robin Graham, Henry Leader (kneeling), David Hobday, Geoffrey Roughton, James Pooler, David Miller, Derek Carr.

There were very few protests against this peaceful confinement but there was an almost fabled incident in the late Thirties when three boys ran away. No one quite knew what sparked the event: it may have been unhappiness and a longing for home but some thought it more likely to have been a prank or dare. It was first light on a summer morning when three escapees sneaked into the bike-shed and quietly peddled off for home. Within a few hours, however, mechanical failure put an end to the attempt when a bicycle chain broke and the unfortunate boy had to be towed by his friends. Eventually the run-aways decided to abandon their break for freedom and to face the consequences rather than to struggle on in such a conspicuous and uncomfortable state of disrepair. Other escapades undertaken included a midnight breakout when two boys got as far as the railway line. When accounts of their escape reached the headmaster he sentenced them to deprivation of sweets for a week.

ORGANISED ENTERTAINMENT

ANYONE INTENDING TO RUN A SUCCESSFUL PREPARATORY SCHOOL required experience in organising leisure activities for the boys such as sport, performances of drama, concerts of music, art, outdoor pursuits and gardening.

As at most schools, plays and concerts were an annual occurrence and substantial effort was put into all aspects of the production. The art teacher was

Programme for a school production of *Snow White* from the early 1930s.

The cast of a school play performed in the early 1950s.

43

ELM PARK: COUNTRY HOUSE TO PREPARATORY SCHOOL

drafted in to paint the scenery and Seth-Smith himself took an avid interest, making sure that everything would happen as it should on the day of the performance. Programmes were printed and the boys spent hours rehearsing their lines. These plays were performed to an invited audience of the boys' parents and on at least one occasion in the last years of the school a professional photographer from Armagh was engaged to record the event.

Some of the boys at the swimming pool *c.*1950.

Boys in the swimming pool under the watchful eye of Putty, *c.*1922.

A programme from December 1948 recorded that the performance was organised by The Elm Park Amateur Dramatic Society. On that occasion the two plays performed by the boys were *The Hordle Poacher* by Bernard Gilbert and *The Warming Pan*, a comedy by W.W. Jacobs.

Sometimes too, outside entertainment would be brought in; the famous conjurer, Ernest Sewell, came and put on shows in the late 1940s and early 1950s.

More conventional contests and pastimes came and went with the seasons. Autumn of course brought conkers and during the spring and summer on hot days model boats were raced on the swimming pool. Strict rules applied in the competition for the Blue Riband, a title borrowed from the famous contest in the 1930s between the great ocean liners for the fastest crossing of the Atlantic. Willow had several model boats of his own. One of these, the *Iolanthe*, was powered by solidified methylated spirit. The swimming pool at Elm Park, as one ex-pupil recalls, 'has moved into folklore. Surrounded by trees and freezing cold the water was completely black. There was a carpet of leaves on the bottom'. Other boys recall the leeches that populated the water and although many certainly learned to swim in it, the sport enjoyed with their model boats seemed more popular.

A more relaxing competitive pursuit was carried out under the patronage of Willow. If a boy expressed an interest, a small patch of ground was set aside to cultivate as a garden. This was tended assiduously throughout the year and a prize was awarded by the masters at the end of term for the best kept garden. Although the prize was usually a nominal one such as a book, competition could be fierce. For instance when parents visited on Saturday afternoons, among the eagerly awaited supplies from the outside world might be small selection of bedding plants to improve the chances of winning the gardening prize. The 'gardens' were of modest dimensions, each about a yard square, sectioned off along a sunny bank. Mr Weaving took a special interest in this activity and some of his letters to old boys mention the front runners for the gardening prize in the same way as the sporting prowess of others: 'Either Morton or Eddie Orr will win the prize. They are running neck and neck at present'.

ORGANISED SPORT

As in all prep schools, sport was an essential part of Elm Park's curriculum. Even at an early stage in the development of prep schools it was generally agreed that organised team sports should be an essential element. If the teachers did not take charge of the organisation of sport in the schools, the pupils themselves would take the initiative and find outlets for their energy that might not always please their elders. When boys were playing for school teams, by contrast, teachers could help them to understand and make allowances for each other's strengths and weaknesses, support each other loyally in action, and enjoy the pleasures that come from playing well. They would gain self-confidence, self-discipline and the ability to co-operate with others in the pursuit of worthwhile goals. Sport would also foster the 'muscular Christianity' that was at the core of the late Victorian concept of manliness and godliness. This philosophy was reflected in a sermon allegedly preached by a headmaster of an Eastbourne prep

A cricket match in progress in the early years.

Cricket team including Peter Hinchcliffe (third from left in back row) and Bobby Bolton (back row extreme right).

school, who explained the concept of the Trinity, not as St Patrick did by using the analogy of the three-leafed shamrock, but with the phrase 'three stumps – one wicket'. Many boys did learn to appreciate the comradeship bred by team games and to treat matches as sporting contests that ended with the final whistle. Sometimes the organisers' good intentions that the competition would encourage character building and gentlemanly traits were forgotten in the heat of competition. And there were of course others bent on profit: one boy remembers being 'told off for running a book on school sports day'.

Cricket was taken very seriously. The cricket pitch was always carefully mowed by Bob Mitchell with a gang mower pulled by 'his invention'. The preparation for, and formality of, a cricket match was very much part of the game and one boy still recalls with astonishment the day a team arrived from Armagh Royal School for a match and 'only two or three boys wore whites!'

FIXTURES.

Day	Date		Opponent			Venue	Result
Sat.,	May	25th	Brackenber House	…	…	Home	Lost They 50 & 8 1st inns us 44
Wed.,	June	5th	Armagh Royal School	…	Home	Scratched
Sat.,	June	8th	Mourne Grange	…	…	Away	Scratched
Wed.,	June	12th	Campbell Coll. Prep. School	Home	……………
Wed.,	June	19th	Rockport	…	…	…	Away	Scratched
Thurs.,	June	27th	Aravon	…	…	…	Away	Scratched
Wed.,	July	3rd	Armagh Royal School	…	Away	Won E.P. A.R.
Thurs.,	July	4th	The Fathers	…	…	Home	Lost E.P.

Elm Park's cricket fixture list for 1935.

During the war when troops were stationed nearby, the famous England left-hand spin bowler, Hedley Verity, visited Elm Park and played with the boys. Once a year there was a cricket match against a team selected from the fathers of the boys.

A letter from Willow written to a boy who had recently left Elm Park in 1937 gives us an insight into the performance of that year's team: 'Of our cricket-matches so far we have lost two and won two. Cabin Hill beat us largely owing to an effective lob-bowler. We ought to have beaten Rockport for ours was obviously the better team, but bad fielding threw the match away. Today the team have just started for Mourne Grange. The weather is so uncertain that I am doubtful whether they will get a game'.

As well as cricket, football and hockey were played at Elm Park. Mr Seth-Smith was a hockey enthusiast and in the early years of the school had been a familiar sight refereeing and indeed playing matches with the boys. It was during the break between lessons in the afternoons that team sports were played, beginning at 2.30p.m. Some of the older boys enjoyed the occasional game of tennis as there was a 'rather mossy grass tennis court with inadequate netting'. It was not supervised by the staff.

Being somewhat isolated from other similar institutions, Elm Park's hockey opponents were sought wherever they could be found. One regular confrontation was against Manor House school situated at Milford near Armagh. The fact that the opposing team were girls a few years older than themselves did not dampen the Elm Park boys' enthusiasm. Indeed as one ex-Manor House girl recalled, the younger more agile boys frequently ran rings round their female opponents. Considering the strictness of the boys' confinement to the school and grounds, gaining a place on a sports team made escape possible, at least temporarily in the form of away matches to other schools.

The other northern prep schools were popular opponents as well and boys fondly recall the attraction of away matches at Mourne Grange near Kilkeel and Rockport at Craigavad. It is remarkable how often the details and result of these matches are ignored for in-depth descriptions of the refreshments on offer to the visiting Elm Parkians. Such a visit to Rockport is recalled: 'We did what we liked till lunch time, then we had dinner (chops, peas, potatoes and jam tart)'. The pitch used for football and hockey matches was grazed by the school's dairy herd and although this was just about adequate for sporting purposes there was always the danger of stepping into what the cows had left behind. For those who had neither aptitude nor interest in sport it meant many long afternoons 'in a field littered with cowpats kicking a heavy, wet leather ball'.

One comment made again and again is the regret that rugby was not played at Elm Park. The resulting lack of experience was sorely felt when the boys arrived at their new public schools, which almost without exception played the game.

Some boys naturally enjoyed games more than others and one boy sums up his indifference thus 'I never much enjoyed any game other than chess … and gave up all other games on leaving school'. In contrast were the many youngsters who enjoyed every aspect of sport. They were impressed by feats such as two boys running 33 times around the 660 yard perimeter of the cricket pitch adding up to twelve and a half miles, just short of a half marathon.

As well as the annual athletics on sports day and team sports there was also regular sessions of physical training, referred to by everyone as 'PT'. During the Thirties this was taken by Mr Sharpley in the 'corn barn'. He adopted the method of playing a song on a gramophone record called 'Why did she follow the leader of the band?', 'and when instructed to perform say 'open feet astride jumping close', you complied but if he said O'Grady says, you did nothing'. During the Second World War the boys drilled with wooden rifles, some thought left over from the 1912 era but other boys imagined they had specially been made for the purpose.

Sports day

Sports day was the highlight of the summer term not just because of the competition for prizes but due rather to the fact that everybody's parents would arrive at the school and so the entire day had a certain carnival atmosphere about it. With the usual variety of athletic competitions, ranging from the high jump to the 100 yards, sports day was one of the occasions, like the end of term matches, when boys proclaimed their allegiance to one or other of the school houses. The White Rose of Lancaster competed against the Red Rose of York.

Looking back many of the boys recall their vehement dislike for the organised sports that made up so much of the school timetable, especially cricket, as compared to their wild antics in the Glen. There was at least one occasion when this frustration seems to have been manifested in direct action. The cricket pavilion was a small building built from a brittle asbestos-like material and one afternoon became the target for a group of stone throwers. The walls were smashed under their barrage of stones and devastated in an orgy of destructive delight. Needless to say the guilty parties were quickly rounded up, severely lectured and heavily fined. Of course young boys do not need any excuse for outbursts of destructiveness and it is just as likely they were not expressing any hatred towards the game of cricket but were just being malicious.

The sheer boredom for someone who hated cricket has been nicely described by a few boys who obviously wished they had been somewhere else. 'I whiled away my summer afternoons as "long-stop" which allowed me to slowly drop out of sight down the slope at the end of the playing fields only to be disturbed by the occasional ball flying over my head.' Sometimes it got to the stage where direct action seemed the only alternative and it was not unheard of for cricket balls to disappear down rabbit holes. It is said this tactic was once used at an away game against Brackenber House when two legendary brothers proved impossible to get out and one wily Elm Park player made the ball mysteriously vanish. Cricket is summarised by one boy as 'an unforgivable waste of endless summer hours'.

Being bad at games could lead not just to apathy but as one boy explained might manifest a loathing of the time wasted playing them. When asked what he disliked most about his time at Elm Park he said 'the perpetual damned games – such a waste of time and distortion of values'. Another boy who admitted to being 'a bit of a rabbit at games' nevertheless entered into the world of 'imaginary cricket' with relish. Played with 'a made up score sheet and two ends from a hexagonal pencil, with the number of runs 1-6 written on one, and bowled/caught/lbw/caught and bowled/run out/not out, on the other.'

Sports day programme for 1932. Obviously the owner was a member of the Red Rose house.

The Glen.

THE GLEN

ALTHOUGH THE NEATLY LAID-OUT GARDENS around the house with their tall trees, manicured lawns and clipped hedges presented a pretty sight to visitors, a hidden wonderland nearby was the preserve of the Elm Park boys. The Glen was the name given to a steep-sided wooded area with its stream that separated Elm Park townland from Tonnagh. It was an exciting and mysterious adventure playground that offered a rustic alternative to the English and Latin lessons. Sunday afternoons were set aside for playing in the Glen when, as one boy put it, 'the mob would invade it'.

Left to right: A. Perceval-Maxwell, [?] Swiney, D.H. Montgomery, [?] Beatty, J. Baxter. *c.*1950.

Although the stream was small the extent to which boys were permitted to wander depended on their swimming ability. 'Full swimmers' were allowed access to the entire glen on both sides of the stream. A full swimmer had achieved this status by swimming a length of Elm Park's swimming pool. 'Half swimmers' could not go over the stream but could venture as far as the icehouse.

The hunter-gatherer instinct prevailed in the Glen and a boy who had 'snares and traps all over the place' remembers catching rabbits and 'guddling' trout in the stream. During the week there was little time to play in the Glen but after lunch and before games started there was usually time to check the rabbit snares. One boy recalls 'roasting rabbit over a wood fire': he does not add, however, that he ate his catch afterwards. In later years the trout probably deserted the stream for healthier waters for when a few boys decided to 'have a quick bathe in the stream' one summer evening they were caught and brought before Seth-Smith. They were given a good telling off and warned not to try something so silly again as the stream was polluted.

The Glen was a wonderful place to observe nature and Mr Weaving would take boys on nature walks there, pointing out species of plants and trees and identifying different birds. One summer in the late Thirties there was a vixen and three cubs patrolling the Glen in the evenings. The boys would often catch glimpses of them from across the stream as the wary animals moved through the rhododendrons and undergrowth. In Mr Weaving's poetry his own deep feelings for the natural world and the changing seasons is strongly conveyed. It is not difficult to imagine him quietly returning to the Glen on those long summer evenings when the boys had abandoned their tree houses for their dormitories, and there quietly composing his poems.

Sunlit trees in late autumn

>The trees have cast their clothes.
>Not a stained clout
>Hangs on a single tree
>In the woods or out.
>
>They that in coloured rags
>Like beggars stood
>All in a night have changed
>Their whimpering mood.
>
>Stripped to the glistening skin
>Naked they stand
>With mighty muscle and thew,
>A glorious band,
>
>Not like slaves that await
>Their masters' rods,

> But wrestlers ready to challenge
> The strength of the Gods.
>
> The trees have cast their clothes:
> Not a fear is theirs.
> Let winter with all his force
> Come when he dares.
>
> With strength of body and joy
> Of heart will they strive
> Till winter fly as in hope
> To escape alive,
>
> And Spring comes in with a shrill
> Triumphant strain
> To crown and garland them
> With her leaves again.
>
> From *Toys of Eternity*, 1937

Of course the Glen's attractions could become addictive and as well as being late back to class there were occasions when impromptu visits were paid en masse to this natural playground. Nobody could remember what prompted it, but one day during the war years 'the whole of shell form (except for one) took off into the Glen'. This class of older boys were meant to have been preparing for one of

The woodcutters' gang seen here equipped with several hatchets gathered fuel for the school fires.

Christopher Cowdy *c.*1944, holding his pet jackdaw.

Mr Barbour's classes and indeed maybe that was reason enough for them to make a bid for freedom. It was in vain, however, for they were all quickly rounded up and given a conduct mark each.

In the early years the boys were content to construct small wooden boats and race them down the stream but later more sophisticated adventurers devised ambitious plans for their own private jungle. Gangs were formed and each busied itself building its headquarters to be defended at all costs from opposing gangs' surprise raids. Saplings were felled and to own a small hatchet became every boy's ambition. Letters home requested that hatchets be posted to the school. Apparently some parents acceded to this unusual request on the grounds that it was an essential piece of equipment for the afternoons spent in the Glen. It might even qualify its owner for an introduction into the woodcutters' gang, an intrepid bunch of boys armed with hatchets and towing a makeshift sleigh gathering wood for the classroom fires and acquiring a certain amount of respect and envy from the younger boys.

The quality of the tree houses they designed and constructed displayed the ingenuity of the boys. Especially during the 1930s some of the tree houses were quite sophisticated pieces of architecture. During the war some of the place-names in the news were applied to these houses and names like Tobruk, Guam and Midway made their way into Elm Park folklore. The houses themselves were not mere shacks but comfortable dwellings: John Cowdy's was strengthened outside with woven bamboo that grew in the Glen and consisted of two storeys. The upper apartments were reserved for the inner circle of gang members and there plans were devised for the next raid against their rivals. The walls were often insulated and chinked with moss making them almost completely weatherproof.

THE GLEN

The Herdman house is still remembered fifty years later as 'a work of art'!

Birds' nests were always going to be attractive targets for young boys and although egg collecting was one motive, there were others. Somehow the boys discovered that with a little patience jackdaw chicks could be reared and tamed and thus emerged the Jackdaw gang. The chicks were hidden away at the back of the 'pavvy' [cricket pavilion] and weaned on wet bread and worms. Jackdaws were by far the easiest birds to tame but a few boys had pet jays and hooded crows and it was not unusual to see several of these birds squawking at dorm windows to be fed by their adopted parents. The birds were sometimes taken home during the summer but away from their familiar surroundings they usually flew away never to return.

There was always meant to be a master supervising the boys in the Glen on Sunday afternoon but that was a thankless and near impossible task. The master on duty was not always up to the job either and an unfortunate and rather eccentric teacher who frequently got this job was mercilessly teased by the boys. Some of the perpetrators admit now that things occasionally went too far. 'When on duty on a Sunday afternoon, he could be persuaded by us, small boys to lie down fully clothed in the river in the Glen!'

Roly Cunningham with his pet Jay.

The fruit pickers
Back row: Alister Perceval-Maxwell, Ralph Cowdy, [?] Caruth, John Swiney, Michael Gordon.
Third row: William Brodie, David Strachan, George Fulton, Anthony Orr, Ian Stoupe, David McMullan, Donn McConnell, Philip Orr.
Second row: Jackson Taggart, Roger Austin, John Chambre, Alan Carson, Miss McQuaide, William Mullan, Peter Acheson.
Front row: David Mongomery, David Lee.

HOME COMFORTS, FOOD AND HEALTH

To the boys, Elm Park was their home for most of the year, so it is important to look at the domestic arrangements. It is entertaining as well as informative to hear what the boys themselves thought of their accommodation and comfort. The preparation element manifests itself again here for it has been suggested that if a boy survived the rigours of prep school then no matter what awaited him at public school it could be faced safe in the knowledge that the worst was behind him. Several elements will be covered in this section including diet, health care and general comfort. We will also look at how the boys coped resourcefully with deficiencies in each of these areas.

Food
The food at the school has been both praised and condemned by the boys who either relished, accepted or detested it. Rationing during the war did nothing to improve meal times. It should not be forgotten that Elm Park was also a farm and had its own dairy herd, Mr Seth-Smith was the prime mover behind the farm. There was a time when it was not uncommon to see milk bottle tops in the Killylea neighbourhood with 'Elm Park farm' stamped on them. Vegetable and fruit gardens provided fresh produce for the kitchens as they had during the previous century for the Blacker-Douglas family. Elm Park tomatoes were sold in Armagh shops but how much of the quality produce filtered down to the boys' dinner table is not known. Judging from some of the comments below, perhaps not a lot.

One petty grievance that several of the old boys still remember is the rule that, legend has it, was established in the very early years of the school. It was said that at breakfast one morning a boy asked a master if he could pass the marmalade. He was immediately and sharply rebuked with the answer that 'boys do not get marmalade': it was for masters only. One of the reasons a place at Willow's table in the mornings was so sought after was that there was a good chance that somebody would be a recipient of one of Willow's bits of toast and marmalade.

Another delicacy that did not make it onto the boys' plates was the guinea fowl that were raised on the school farm. The only benefit the birds ever provided for the boys was a welcome diversion from schoolwork when they would flock around and perch outside the classroom windows.

Tuck from home of course could provide choice morsels but it was really meant to be shared out so unless well hidden could not always be called upon in times of need. Another risky alternative was 'unauthorised visits to the kitchen'.

If it was impossible to get near the kitchen for a snack between meals, a more daring predatory excursion however could be made through the conservatory. The goal was a few slices of bread and butter from the dining room beyond the French windows where the tables were laid out for the staff at teatime. As one who must have made this foray more than once advised, 'it required speed and nerve'. Another source of nourishment, though probably the least digestible as well as being the most difficult to obtain, were the dog biscuits for Putty's spaniel. These snacks of questionable flavour were occasionally spirited from the conservatory by dedicated teams of boys after lights out. A boy who spent just two terms at Elm Park which he described as 'the most terrible terms of my whole education experience', tried to cheer himself up while there by stealing sweets from one of the school mistresses. He crept into Mrs Fleming's bedroom and had just pinched the goodies when the teacher returned. He could hardly have selected his victim less wisely for red-haired Mrs Fleming was notoriously quick tempered and when she returned unexpectedly, he panicked. 'She came in, I hid under the bed, she went out, so did I'. Having apparently escaped unscathed he was inevitably caught when the evidence in the form of sweet wrappers were found in his pyjama pockets.

The skills and knowledge gained from the boys' pursuits in the Glen could also be used to supplement their diet. Occasionally their knowledge of the natural world proved valuable as the following incident that took place in the Thirties shows. Two boys observed Miss Sewell, the matron, haggling over the price of a salmon with a man who had turned up at the doors of the school with the over-sized fish across the bar of his bicycle. Only for the timely intervention of the boys she would have bought the fish not knowing that the salmon was in fact a pike.

If the food was basic at least a good deal of it was home grown and if the bread was sometimes stale there always seemed to be plenty of it. At least that is the recollection of one boy who also remembers bacon and eggs for breakfast and 'plenty of roasts' at dinner-time. Considering this was during the war and comparing it with what other boys recall of the Elm Park diet, it seems a little embellished but cannot be discounted completely. Certainly if we look at Cyril Ward's diary where he recorded the last Sunday dinner of the 1935 summer term the food was quite good. 'Last Sunday of term. Dinner at night, Grapefruit, Chicken, Meringues, Jelly, Ginger Jelly, Apples, Oranges, Raspberries, Bananas, Chochl[t] Ginger …'

In contrast to the boy above who recalled the nice breakfasts, another who attended after the war had a very different opinion of the food. He said the food 'was absolutely dreadful … I remember being made to eat liver that was covered in some sort of green slime. I have never been able to eat liver since'. If the terrible liver was hard to swallow then the gristle on the 'appalling meat from our

HOME COMFORTS, FOOD AND HEALTH

The dining room with fine mantelpiece and basic furniture. The painting above was The Shannon & the Chesapeake.

eight penny meat ration' proved impossible. Simply spitting it out was not an option under the severe eyes of the watching masters. Having the advantage of fifty years to soften the memory the boy involved wrote that he 'used to retain pieces in my cheek like a hamster until I could get rid of it privately!'

Although admitting that the food at Elm Park was 'pretty terrible', a boy who spent a long career in the Merchant Navy was grateful for his introduction to basic fare. In later life he was happy to eat whatever he was given. Unfortunately not everyone could grin and bear it and the same boy remembers others with more delicate palates 'being left for ages facing plates of cabbage and sprouts'. He may have been able to endure relentless rounds of 'milk puddings and macaroni cheese without cheese' but he also thought it was all 'pretty dreadful'.

Occasional exceptions were made in the regular monotony of the school food. When one boy complained to his parents about the Monday morning flapjacks that he hated being made to eat for breakfast, his mother intervened. The matron was consulted and to the intense jealousy of his friends an egg was cooked especially for him.

Special occasions such as sports day at the end of the summer term called for

ELM PARK: COUNTRY HOUSE TO PREPARATORY SCHOOL

a change from the routine fare and one boy remembers this as the occasion when he first encountered asparagus. Other national holidays were celebrated in a similar way. A picnic on the banks of the Blackwater River is recalled with pleasure by many and may have been to celebrate George V's Jubilee. Another boy remembers his birthday 'celebrated with a feast of strawberries and cream, held in the great conservatory'.

Food, like marbles, cigarette cards and comics was a valid currency at Elm Park and like any currency could rise and fall in value. The novelty of a large tin of Cape Gooseberry jam brought from home by a boy at start of term quickly wore off when those who swapped their own treats for a portion found that the jam tasted of nothing in particular. Like those magic pots so popular in fairy tales, the owner found to his disappointment that the gooseberry jam seemed to last forever.

Because the boys were restricted to the school grounds they depended on weekend visits and parcels from their parents as the only source of sweets and other treats. Dinky cars, torch batteries or whatever the current craze was, elicited requests for these treasures from home. A typical example reads, 'I am getting very excited for the 25th of October bring a whole lot of sweets for I am going to give a dorm feast. David McMullan has been rather cheeky to-day so I hit him hard and told him not to be'. However there was one occasion when an unannounced and unconventional arrival of a package of goodies caused quite a stir. During the war the father of one of the boys who was connected with Aldergrove air base flew over the school and parachuted a package of sweets on to the cricket pitch to the understandable frantic excitement of all the boys.

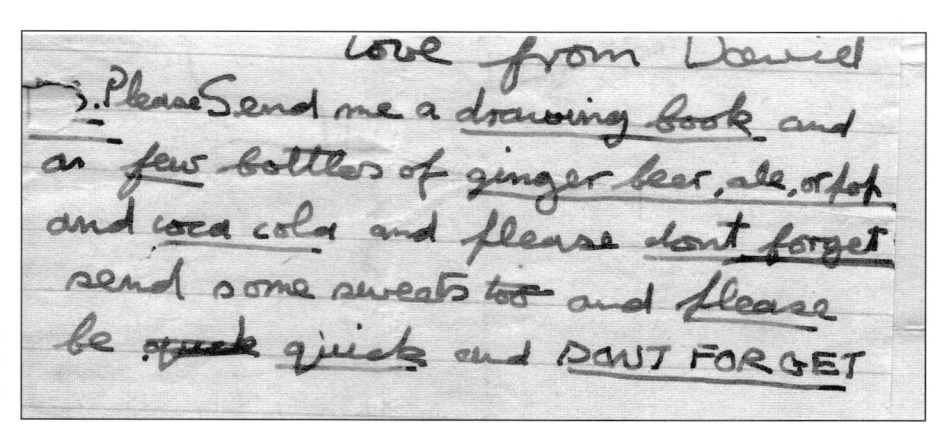

David McMullan who attended Elm Park from 1946.

Extract from a letter written by David Strachan to his parents 29 June 1949 with urgent requests for sweets and Coca-Cola.

HOME COMFORTS, FOOD AND HEALTH

Considering the extent of dissatisfaction with the Elm Park diet and that many boys ate less during term-time than during holidays at home, it was perhaps an unwise policy the school adopted early on of weighing and measuring boys at start and end of term. Many would lose weight only to go home and return next term 'fattened up'.

Some may have complained about the food but others were simply happy that there always seemed to be plenty to eat, admitting that 'we obviously moaned about it but it was pretty good'.

Sickness

With so many young boys living in proximity it was inevitable that common colds and other childhood illnesses would spread if not kept in check. The matron was always the first point of contact but there were occasions when more urgent medical attention was needed. A septic wound from a nail in a football boot needed a visit to the county infirmary in Armagh. Another boy fell from the tree in Trinac and Dr Deane was on hand to set the broken arm; the casualty earned the notoriety of being the first boy to break a bone at the school.

The matter-of-fact treatment that some boys received there is still remembered with a painful shudder. The resident surgeon at Armagh infirmary, Dr Deane was not renowned for his reluctance in wielding the scalpel and he drained the poison from an infected finger by lancing it in such a way that the wound never healed properly. If for some Dr Deane was to be feared, others looked forward to his regular visits. Once he left the school in such a hurry that he swung his car around too fast on the gravel driveway and the vehicle actually overturned.

The type of treatments available were the usual household remedies of the time: iodine and extract of malt were among the everyday contents of the

Elm Park School, main entrance c.1950.

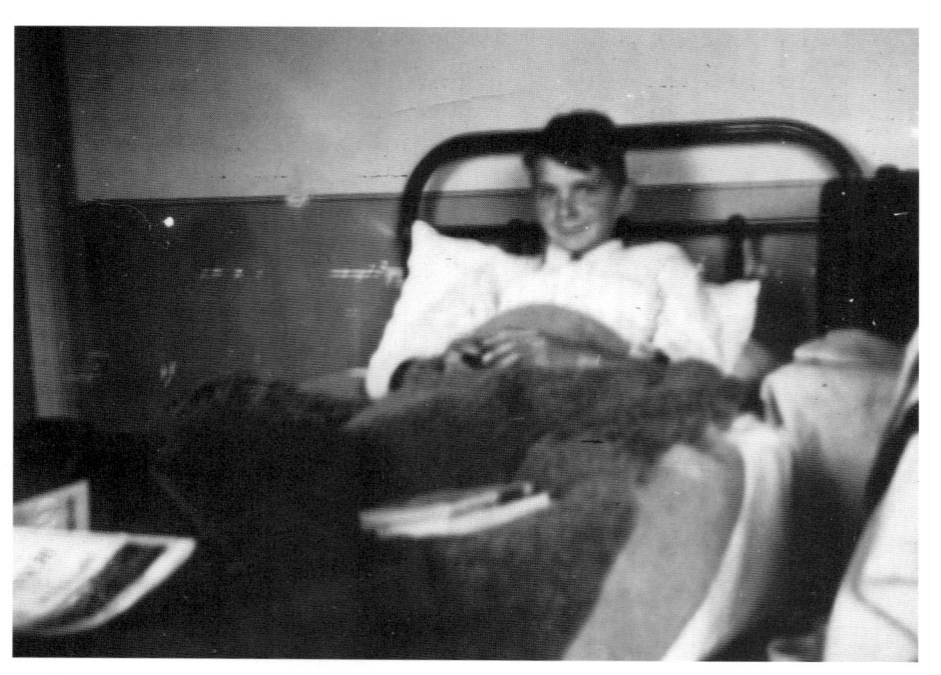

Geoffery Sadlier in sick room taken by Robin Allport in June 1948.

medical cabinet. Another boy tells us that 'we had Radio malt and Minidex every day'.

There were however occasions when neither matron nor Dr Deane could be of any use. One time Mr Seth-Smith took the unusual step of bringing a boy to a local traditional healer. The boy suffered from warts on his hand and clearly remembers meeting 'an old man with a white beard' who charmed the warts away. Although the process itself was not recalled it is clearly remembered that within a fortnight not one wart was left.

It was inevitable that there would be outbreaks of the usual childhood diseases such as chickenpox and measles and depending on the extent of the contagion, dormitories could be converted into isolated sick bays. There was a serious outbreak of measles in 1937 during which Tewkesbury Dorm was turned into a darkened sick bay for the afflicted boys. At such times extra medical aid was needed and the gloomy monotony of the curtained dorm was broken only by occasional visits by 'the bat'. This was the nickname given by the spotted patients to 'a very beautiful night nurse' who attended them.

A few years later during an outbreak of chickenpox Wakefield Dorm was the isolation ward for about three weeks during which time neither friends nor lessons disturbed the patients. The pursuit that fought off the interminable boredom on such occasions was the ever-popular card schools. Although everyone was inoculated against whooping cough a boy who managed to catch it was kept apart from everyone else until he became well again. However the matron allowed him pretty free run of the place as long as he stayed on his own and the kitchen garden became one of his favourite haunts. The surfeit of fresh fruit he consumed during one of these visits had unpleasant after-effects that

HOME COMFORTS, FOOD AND HEALTH

taught him moderation. He spent another part of his time in isolation pursuing an altogether more constructive and artistic goal. There were just four records in the sickroom and by repeatedly playing one of them he learned 'Abdul Abulbul Amir' by heart, and to celebrate his release back among his peers he regaled the entire dormitory with a rendition of the Frank Crumit hit.

The treatment for measles might not have extended much beyond isolation in a darkened environment and one boy who had quite a serious attack was taken home. His father who was a doctor threatened to remove him from school altogether and criticised Elm Park's medical care. Another boy who attended during the same period although not telling us anything specific about conditions recalls complaining often but in vain to his parents. 'It was only' he laments 'when I contracted dysentery that my parents realised that some of the things I had said … were correct.' After a short spell recuperating in the Royal Victoria Hospital he was sent to another school in what his parents hoped was a healthier environment.

Here is a rare contribution to the school magazine by Cyril Ward that versifies an apparently self-inflicted bout of illness. The 'magazine' only existed as a single handwritten copy so there are probably no copies now in existence.

> There was a boy whose name was Hill
> Who told the matron he felt ill
> She straight away sent him off to bed
> Where he complained of a sore head
> The masters were extremely sorry
> And told his mother not to worry
> For in a day or two they said
> Young Hill will surely leave his bed
> The next day Hill was down again
> Without a vestage [sic] of the pain.

A diary entry by Ward on 16 June 1935 gives us a cryptic explanation of the background to the poem. 'John Hill goes to bed as a result of fizzy Lemonade, EXAMS or Campbell's ices.'

Chilly weather
Like any house of a similar size and age Elm Park was not adequately heated as we understand the term today. The rooms with their high ceilings and the draughty corridors only added to the winter chill. The winter of 1947 was notoriously cold and that episode has remained vivid in the memories of many who spent it at Elm Park. The water in the jugs carried up to the dormitories by the maids every morning quickly dropped to the temperature of the surroundings. Some accounts maintain that it froze in the jugs on some occasions. Other times boys used to go to bed fully dressed. Sometimes they even

took the thin mats from the dorm floors and added them to their bedclothes. Only when some of the boys in a particular dormitory were suffering from colds or influenza was the luxury conceded of having a fire lit in the morning. Other discomforts that the boys attributed to cold weather and poor diet were chilblains, impetigo and boils.

Although the dormitories had no heating except when occasionally fires were lit, some of the more modern classrooms near the conservatory did have central heating. The library and big schoolroom too were always heated during the winter by log fires. They were not really effective enough to save the boys at the back of the room from suffering.

Anthony Orr and Ralph Cowdy tobogganing on the hill below the playing fields.

ACADEMIC STANDARDS

Boys were sent to Elm Park to be prepared for education in public schools in England or Ireland and so its curriculum was designed to get boys through the Common Entrance Examination and prepare them for life in the public school system. All the boys went on to public school in England, to an Irish equivalent such as Campbell College in Belfast or St. Columba's outside Dublin, or else to the Royal Naval College at Dartmouth. The subjects taught therefore included Greek, Latin, French, English, mathematics, history, geography, divinity, drawing and music.

Some boys were beginning to resent what they considered to be undue emphasis on the classics but in these circumstances they were fortunate to have an English teacher of the quality of Willow. Typical of the type of teaching that

A typical end of term report. Note the conduct marks recorded bottom left and the boy's height and weight at the beginning and end of term, recorded top right.

Willow was best remembered for, was his general knowledge class in the library which one imagines must have been the kind of free form question-and-answer session beloved of boys curious for knowledge. Much knowledge was committed to memory whether it was Latin declensions, the names and dates of the kings and queens of England, or quantities of English poetry: not perhaps the most imaginative approach but much appreciated by many of them in later life. Although science was not taught there were occasional visits from lecturers whose topics included natural history, travel and geography supplemented with a film or magic lantern show.

Another valuable weekly exercise was LMN, a mental arithmetic test. Two dozen questions had to be answered in forty minutes. Only the quicker, bright boys could hope to achieve full marks three weeks in a row and so qualify for exemption from the following week's test. Many others, however, sharpened their skills in the kind of practical exercise that would prove useful in adult life long after the complexities of Latin grammar had been forgotten.

One of the most valuable practices in the school was the provision to parents of a weekly report slip with up to the minute facts on the progress or otherwise of each boy. These supplemented the usual end of term reports. These reports included sections where conduct was graded and it was noted if any stars had been awarded during the previous seven days for 'proficiency in work'. Such individual attention was possible only with small numbers of pupils in each class.

Some of the boys in Form 4, taken by Robin Allport in 1948.

The library in which Willow had his classes for senior boys and which had a range of appropriate books.

ELM PARK: COUNTRY HOUSE TO PREPARATORY SCHOOL

The quality of the education provided at Elm Park should be judged against the aims of the school and how the boys fared when they entered public school. In general they found that they were able to hold their own when competing against pupils across the Irish Sea. A successful pupil summed up Elm Park academically when he said it was 'effective if not too ambitious'. A typical comment runs: 'I had a good grounding in all subjects'. Indeed, what comes across from reading through the comments of those who attended Elm Park is that rather than emphasising any single academic accolade, most boys left with improved self-esteem. When trying to describe what they gained at Elm Park they mention terms like 'independence', 'resourcefulness', 'manners' and 'values'. Some even believe they had become more 'streetwise'. They confirm the old dictum: 'A preparatory school should be a nursery for hardening young cuttings, not a hot-house to force exotic plants'.

An example of the kind of arithmetic problems the boys were regularly expected to solve.

TEACHING STAFF

Headmasters

The backbone of the teaching staff at Elm Park were the two founding headmasters who took many of the older boys and specialised in subjects such as French and Greek. In most prep schools it was common that the youngest boys were taught by female teachers and Elm Park followed this trend. Boys of seven or eight could feel alienated and find it hard to come to terms with long spells away from home among strangers. The presence of a teacher who was also a maternal figure could be a great comfort. There were also various assistant masters, some of whom stayed for long periods and others who came and went with the terms. Many of the teachers who passed through Elm Park in this capacity were either young men and women looking for experience or older and sometimes unusual characters looking for a situation. There were also visiting teachers for subjects such as music, art and carpentry.

The subjects taught at Elm Park were dictated by the function of the institution. Because boys were being prepared for life in the public school system there was a natural emphasis on the classics and a reluctance to spend time on science.

The Seth-Smith/Weaving team was dynamic, with each complementing the other. After Seth-Smith's death in 1946 a lot of the dynamism vanished. The influence later of Mr Williams was a strong one – he was 'a most effective teacher and well liked', but the affinity that had existed between the two World War One comrades just could not be rejuvenated in the new post-World War Two partnership.

Teachers

In the early years of the school when there were very few boys the two headmasters were all that was needed but when numbers rose in the late 1920s it became necessary to think of employing teachers. A female teacher for the young boys was one of the first additions to the staff. Miss Irwin taught for a few years between 1923 and 1925.

In 1926 two masters came to Elm Park, Mr G.B. Forge and Mr E. Owen. At the time of writing the latter is still alive although now the quite elderly retired Bishop of Limerick. During the late 1920s Mr J.W. Hunter-Blair and Mr E.W. Coleman joined the staff and Miss Fanning seems to have filled Miss Irwin's post for she appears in 1926. By 1930 with a school student population hovering around thirty boys another master joined the staff, Mr G.A. Willans.

Mr Vernon Farley taught from 1931–36 and for his stay was valued as a music teacher among other things. He was a 'nice friendly master' who was remembered teaching the younger boys Latin. He also took piano lessons and organised some of the concerts and other musical events put on as entertainment from time to time. For instance, he was musical director of the school's production of *The Pirate of Panora* in 1932.

Around this time too Mr C.D. Britten and Mr E.N. Sharpley joined the staff: the latter is remembered as a very big man. By 1937 Mr Harold Clayton (1936-45) was also teaching at the school. He stayed until the mid-1940s and like Farley doubled as music teacher. Clayton arrived at Elm Park as a young man from university and some boys thought him 'rather brash'. He was a short man and ill health prevented him serving during the war: this nevertheless did not prevent certain boys 'wondering aloud' when 'Tubby' Clayton would join up. After his time at Elm Park Clayton collaborated with D.N. Straker and published a school book called *A Natural Approach to Mathematics*.

On the eve of war a substantial increase in the number of new boys, was matched by an increase in staff numbers. However, due to the uncertainty that war brought, there was now an increased turnover in staff. Mrs Ena Fleming, Miss Oliver and Miss Foster came and went in succession. Miss Oliver was 'very blonde' and wore blue eye shadow. She injected a certain air of sophistication into the country school and that perhaps came from her habit of smoking black cat cigarettes. When the war started she left to become a mail censor. Miss Foster taught the younger boys Latin. She was the type of motherly lady 'of mature years' that suited the younger boys so well and was remembered as being very 'nice'. The only record of any science being taught at Elm Park was in Miss Foster's class when it is recalled that she instructed the boys how to draw a cross section of a primrose flower. Not all the female teachers were as well liked as Miss Foster. Miss Fleming is best remembered for her red hair and her equally fiery temper. Her nickname was 'Boygen' or 'Spizboygen'. When she caught one of the boys 'skinny dipping' in the swimming pool she marched him up to the front door of the school with his clothes bundled under his arm. Other boys got on well with her and John Cowdy corresponded with her for many years.

Mr Redmond Barbour was one of the familiar faces among the wartime staff at Elm Park. Nicknamed Ali Barber, he was a tall and short-sighted scholarly man and had a pleasant personality but had problems maintaining discipline. A clergyman who helped out during his time as Rector of Killylea was the Rev. Dickie King. He taught Latin, Greek and Scripture and was a jolly man who is remembered for his enthusiasm on the football pitch. He left Elm Park during the war to become chaplain in the army.

In September 1945 just after the war ended Robin Allport came to Elm Park as a replacement for Mr Clayton. He taught a variety of subjects including Latin,

Three members of the teaching staff outside the conservatory, c.1940. Left to right: H.W. Clayton, Redmond Barbour and Mrs Ena Fleming.

English and History but was remembered by some as specialising in mathematics. The boys knew him affectionately as Olly Allport. He left at the end of the summer term 1948. According to Allport the staff working at Elm Park during the period from 1939-48 were: Mrs E. Fleming, the matron Miss Sewell and Miss Simpson. Miss Leslie McEndoo, daughter of the Dean of Armagh visited the school regularly to teach art and in January 1947 surprised her colleagues by marrying the Archbishop of Armagh, Primate Gregg. Another female teacher from around 1950 was Miss Burrows.

Mr Weaving's brother Montague had taught at the school first in 1938. He was disabled and used a wheelchair and the boys always found him cheerful and 'nice and approachable'. He had spent time working in Canada and the boys loved to hear him regale them with ripping yarns of the frozen north. After the death of Mr Seth-Smith in the winter of 1946 he returned to the school and helped out to a great extent in that difficult period. He became one of the directors, with Michael Williams and Mr Weaving, of Elm Park Ltd. in 1947. Monty Weaving's wife also came to work at the school; she was employed helping with housekeeping and secretarial duties. Unfortunately Monty Weaving died at the beginning of 1950 after being unwell for the previous six months.

During the late 1940s and early 1950s a young David Hannon taught briefly at Elm Park. It was his impressive sports car that stuck in the minds of some of his pupils. He later became a well-known television producer with the BBC.

A rather eccentric master who drifted into the school during its latter years was George Lowdell. In class he was very strict and was known to have rapped a few knuckles for bad behaviour. He seemed to be the brunt of many of the boys' jokes but found it harder to cope with them. One boy remembers him as a 'rather sad figure'. It is doubtful if the discipline he meted out in class was effective. He was said to have kept a slipper for such purposes which he called 'little Jacob' and which he used 'very lightly in combination with a sweet'.

Mr Jacob Baker taught during the mid-Forties too and his brother Esau also taught for a short time in 1945. He only stayed a term and was replaced by Jack Simpson from Cork. Mr Reid was teaching at Elm Park in 1952. The boys knew him as 'Annie' Reid because of his pronunciation of the question after each lesson, 'Annie questions'.

Woodwork, Art and Music
Like music and art, woodwork was one of the optional extras at Elm Park. From the mid-1930s until the late 1940s Dick Hodgett, who it is thought came from Tandragee, taught the subject in one of the yard buildings. Before Mr Hodgett, local man Johnny Linton had taken the woodwork class: his family had long associations with Elm Park going back to the Blacker-Douglas days. One of the masters, Mr Allport, recalled that during his time at the school the boys constructed a 'rather splendid canoe' in the carpentry class.

There was not always a specialist music teacher. In that case the teacher who displayed the most musical talent took responsibility. In the 1930s Mr Farley followed by Mr Clayton filled this role and in the final years of the school Reginald West, the organist in Armagh Cathedral, became the visiting music teacher.

However there were several visiting art teachers over the years. Miss McCordock paid weekly visits to the school from her home in Armagh during the late 1930s. She helped out in other ways too and designed the scenery for the school's 1932 production of *The Pirate of Panora*. Mercy Hunter, the well-known artist and wife of sculptor George McCann, visited the school and took art classes during the period when the couple lived outside Portadown at Vinecash. It is worth recording, however, that John Luke, the Belfast artist, never taught at Elm Park during the war years when he lived with the Terris family at the old Johnston seat of Knappagh which butted onto the Elm Park demesne. After the war Miss McEndoo came to the school once a week as visiting art mistress. In the early 1950s the artistic talents of Trevor Cox were also utilised when he taught art among other subjects. Cox was an accomplished sculptor but later found a much wider audience for his writing talents under the name William Trevor. His wife Jane Cox was also employed at the school, doing bookkeeping and other administrative tasks.

SCHOOL OF '23

Back row: A.L.M. Davidson, W.B. Smyth, C.C. Gotto, F.N. Miller, W.G. Carson, E.O. Greeves, R.C. Roe, E. Robb, J.B. Wylie.
Second row: J.O. Wylie, Miss Irwin, H.W. Weaving, Esq., H.E. Seth-Smith, Esq., Miss Seymour, B. Kelly.
Front row: B. Steen, G.D. Stevenson, F.C. Gotto, E. Dorman, J.K. Rogers, J.B. Pears.

SCHOOL OF '28

Back row: B. Woods, W. Hurst, R. Faris, S. Henderson, L. Rentoul, H. Millar, J. Lytle, D. Woods, R. McDonald, A. Millar.
Third row: G. Carey, P. Dorman, R. Stewart, D. Williams, T. Adair, F. Mann, G. Stevenson, H. Thomson, D. Ross.
Second row: R. Walsh, W.E. Coleman, Esq., Miss Fanning, H.W. Wearing, Esq., H.E. Seth-Smith, Esq., Miss Cranston, R. Workman.
Front row: J. Preston, I. Ewart, T. Cowdy, S. Millar, C. Beatty, R. Yarr.

SCHOOL OF '30

Back row: T. Cowdy, R. Scott, E. Cooke, P. Horsbrugh, D. Woods, A. Millar, F. Stephens, W. McDonald, A. Gore-Booth.
Third row: R. Yarr, R. McDonald, S. Millar, B. Woods, J. Lytle, S. Henderson, E. Smyth, T. Bulloch, A.S. Henderson, W. Hurst.
Second row: D. Williams, H. Millar, G.B. Forge, Esq., H.W. Weaving, Esq., H.E. Seth-Smith, Esq., E. Owen, Esq., Miss Cranston, L. Lytle, R. Faris.
Front row: C. Ward, J. Carson. Absent: K. Millar, N. Stewart, B. Cowdy, R. Magill.

SCHOOL OF '32

Back row: B. Cowdy, A. Gore-Booth, C. Ward, G. Dougan, F. Stephens, L. Plunkett, B. McDonald, R. Magill, T. Dickson, N. Stuart, A. Medlock.
Third row: T. Hurst, E. Cook, P. Horsbrugh, R. Scott, B. Woods, F. Smyth, S. Henderson, S. Millar, R. Yarr, K. Millar, R. Morton.
Second row: G. Lyttle, V. Farley, Esq., G. Willans, Esq., H.W. Weaving, Esq., H.E, Seth-Smith, Esq., Miss Cranston, T. Cowdy, W. Hurst.
Front row: J. Hill, J. Carson, J.J. Hill, P. Adeley, B. Duffin, T. Haughton.

SCHOOL OF '35

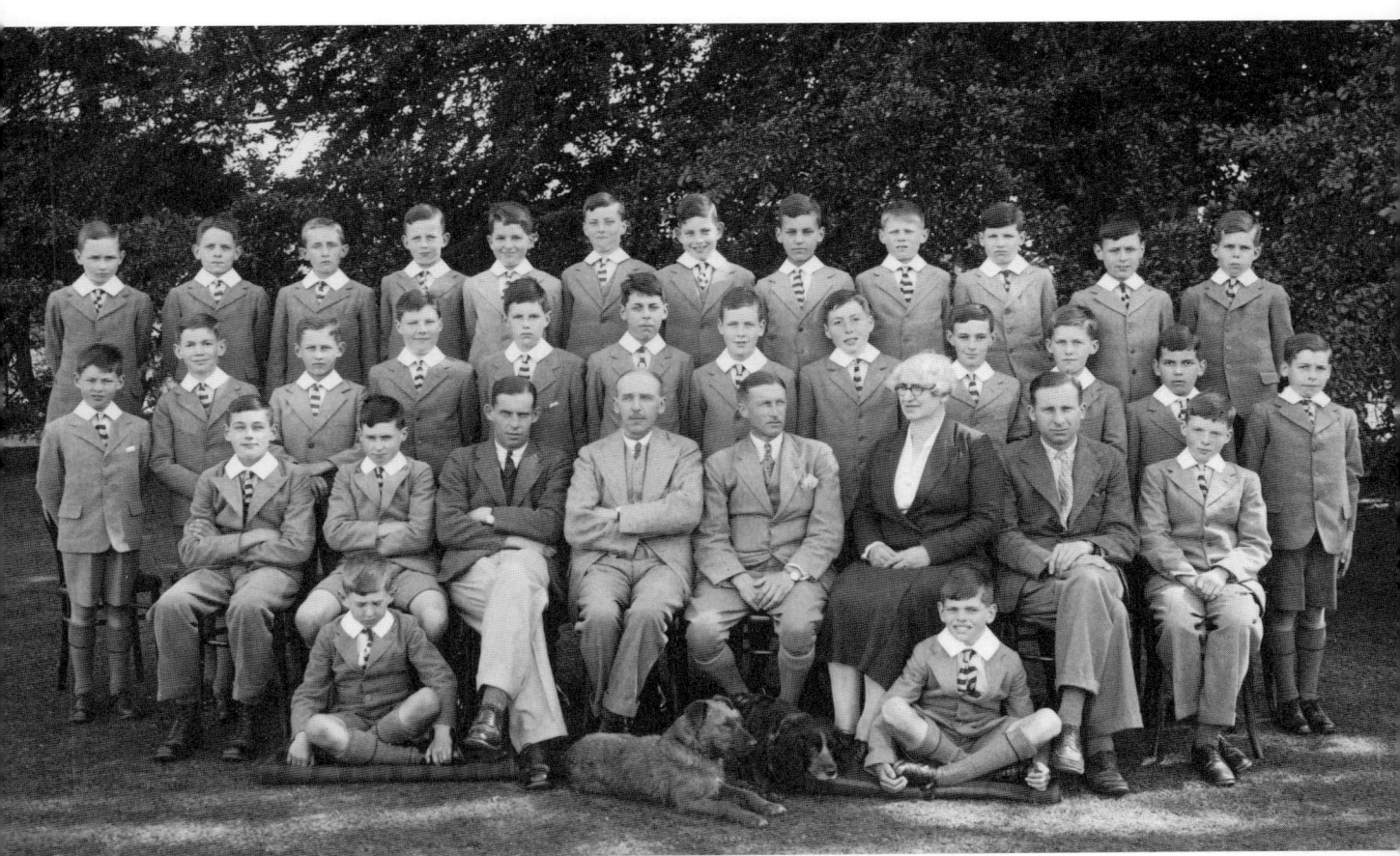

Back row: J.J. Hill, B. Duffin, J. Hill, G. Workman, B. Faulkner, D. Woods, C. Cowdy, S. Good, D. Hardy, C. Stewart, F. McCance, R. Charley.
Third row: S. Dickson, T. Haughton, H. Good, A, Medlock, D. MacLeay, L. Plunkett, B. Scott, E. Orr, R. Morton, P. Adeley, D. Jamison, M. Campbell.
Second row: C. Ward, T. Hurst, C.D. Britten, Esq., H.W. Weaving, Esq., H.E. Seth-Smith, Esq., Miss MacDonald, V.D. Farley, Esq., T. Dickson.
Front row: M. Mackie, H. Crawford.

SCHOOL OF '37

Back row: I. Wilson, N. Ferguson, H. Crawford, C. Proctor, B. Ross, B. Rees, R. Charley, A. Henderson, J. Cowdy, M. Mackie, J. Kinnaird, H. Knox-Browne, H. Stevenson.
Third row: J. Hill, F. McCance, M. Campbell, J. Carr, C. Cowdy, I. Workman, D. Hardy, D. Jamison, J. Pringle, S. Dickson, R. Carson.
Second row: E. Orr, D. Woods, H.W. Clayton, Esq., H.W. Weaving, Esq., H.E. Seth-Smith, Esq., Miss MacDonald, E.N. Sharpley, Esq., S. Good, D. Mac
Front row: A. Knighton Smith, A. Fforde, G. Fitz-Gibbon, J. Duquid, R. Turner, V. Whyte, R. Hill, N. McCance.

SCHOOL OF '45

Back row: Robert Bell, Hugh Acworth, Roderick McRea, Ion Montgomery, Patrick Montgomery, Hugh Montgomery, Peter McMullan, Tom Crozier, H.P. Lindsay, Malcolm Crawford, Jamie Stuart, Angus McConnell, David Maitland-Titterton, James Leslie.
Second row: Henry Mulholland, Christopher Cowdy, Garry Campbell, Oliver Paton, Robert Morton, Donald Weir, Roly Cunningham, Robin Sadlier, Mark Herdman, Pat Darragh, Robert Barrett, Tim Sinton, Terance Darling.
First row: Charlie Stewart, Michael Faris, Arthur Nugent, Mr. Baker, Mrs Fleming, Mr H.W. Weaving, Mr H.E. Seth-Smith, Mrs Sewell, Mr R. Allport, James Stronge, Brian Faris, Michael Turner.
Seated on ground: Franklin Cardy, Martin Proctor, Lindsay Finney, Geoffry Sadlier, Godfrey Weir, Hugh Stewart.

SCHOOL OF '49

Back row: Patrick Taylor, George Fulton, Simon Haselden, David Strachan, Bobby Boulton, Alastair Percival-Maxwell, John Graham, John Burrell, Michael Gordon, John Bruce, Bill Mullan, Edward Orr, Teddy Graham, Anthony Orr.
Second row: Bill Jackson, Donn McConnell, Peter Acheson, Franklin Cardy, John Cunningham, Owen French, Henry Armstrong, John Armstrong, Paul Hillis, Robert Arnold, Martin Proctor, David McMullan.
First row: Michael Haselden, Lindsey Finney, Miss ffrench-Eager, Mr M. Weaving, Mrs M. Weaving, Mr W. Weaving, Mr M. Williams, Miss Shea, Mr Harris, John Lee, Peter Robin Hinchcliffe.
Seated on ground: John Greig, Bill Montgomery, Tony Wilkinson, Edward Bird, Edward Beattie, Ian Stoupe, Ralph Cowdy, Robin Hillis, John Swiney.

SCHOOL OF '53

Back row: M.J.P. Browne, M. Acheson, G.E.C. Beatty, B.M. Gordon, A. Topping, D.G. Lee, W A. Carson, WH. Brodie.
Middle row: C. Caruth, J.M. Fulton, R.E. Cowdy, W.E. Russell, J.A. Chambre, P.C. Orr, T.A.W. Wilkinson, J.I.Irwin.
Seated: J.L. Baxter, Miss Kells, Mrs Jane Cox, Mr T. Cox Esq., Mr M. Williams Esq., Mrs M. Williams, Mr J.C.F. Smyth Esq., R.I. Stoupe, G.O. Fulton.
Seated on ground: R. Blundell, D.A. McManus, B. Blundell, C.A. Stoupe.

NON-TEACHING STAFF

Matrons

Mention has also to be made of the matrons who throughout the years of the school were a series of unsung heroines staving off epidemics of measles and chickenpox and dealing with all sorts of domestic accidents and disasters. They indeed were the maternal figurehead at Elm Park.

Elm Park's first matron was Miss Seymour (1921-25) followed in 1926 by Miss Cranston who remained until 1933. She died on 13 February of that year.

Miss McDonald became matron after Miss Cranston's death. Like her predecessor she was from Scotland but unlike her she was a large woman and was given the unkind nickname of Doodly. It was claimed that she had an aversion to pupils by the name of Campbell dating back to the massacre of Glencoe. One of the main concerns of the matron on her daily rounds was to ensure that the bowels of every boy had moved that day, and mimics of this nightly lavatorial roll call performed with a strong Scottish accent were sure to provoke much amusement. The matron's nightly inquiries were complemented each morning by Mr Seth-Smith's familiar inquiry about the brushing of teeth.

Miss McDonald was succeeded by Miss Phyllis Sewell. She 'was well liked but had a firm hand', a good character reference for any matron. During her time at the school she had married a foreign gentleman, Mr Koczeban, and left with him in the mid-1940s. The red-haired teacher, Mrs Fleming, had a sister, Miss Megaw who became matron when Miss Sewell left. She came to the school from Lowther College and held that post during the period 1945-47.

Another matron who did not stay very long was Miss Nutter. She arrived some time during the war and it seems preceded Miss Shea. There may have been other matrons between these two for one boy recalls a matron called Miss Bronwell.

Miss Molly Shea was the last of Elm Park's matrons; she came there about 1948 and in 1951 married the joint headmaster Michael Williams. She was assisted by a Miss McDowell and later by Yvonne Acheson. Miss Mair also acted as assistant matron to Miss Shea and Miss Patience Leader lent a hand in a variety of ways and could also fall into this role. As the latter lady said herself, 'I did whatever was required of me – feeding ducks – flower arranging – darning and patching and dishing out porridge'.

NON-TEACHING STAFF

Household and outdoor staff

Complementing the teachers there were the strong and reliable team of workers that insured the whole institution ran smoothly. Some of the men who worked in the gardens and farm had long family connections with the house going back to the Blacker-Douglas days. There was also a full complement of household staff, for the school operated in many ways like a large extended family. When Mr Seth-Smith visited friends one of the men would act as chauffeur. In the latter days of the school Alfie Connelly looked after all things mechanical and basically maintained the building, surroundings and Mr Seth-Smith's car. Cecil Bruce looked after much of the grounds and James McIlveen cared for the cattle among other things.

The female staff responsible for the smooth day-to-day running of the school were a crucial part of its history. For instance there were the maids who made the boys' beds, darned their socks and scrubbed their grubby knees when they returned from the Glen. The cook and kitchen staff who, despite some of the culinary horror stories from the boys, were generally appreciated and made the best with what resources they had available. One boy's very last letter to his parents before he left Elm Park for good was full of specific instructions for them to send him some money so that he could leave tips for the maids. 'This is VERY IMPORTANT so send off 25/- as quickly as possible, it must arrive before next Tuesday…Again VERY IMPORTANT.'

In the early days Bob Mitchell was the mainstay behind the smooth running of many of the day-to-day aspects of school life. Everything from providing the logs that burned in the classroom fires to maintaining the cricket pitch was his domain. It was Bob who used his mechanical expertise to create 'the invention' built around the engine and chassis of a Morris Cowley from the 1920s. It performed essential functions as various as pulling the mower on the cricket pitch and transporting the boys' trunks from Killylea railway station to the

Bob Mitchell and his invention, with a group of enthusiastic helpers, *c*.1940.

school and back again each term. This indispensable vehicle was disliked by Mr Seth-Smith who preferred traditional horse-drawn transport. Of course tradition would have required much more work from Mr Mitchell and his men. Before the introduction of Mr Mitchell's invention the mower had indeed been horse-drawn and to stop the horses cutting up the turf, they had had to wear special leather shoes. Joseph Lutton had managed such tasks when he had worked for the Blacker-Douglas family prior to the opening of the school. Some boys understood the importance of Mr Mitchell's contribution to the success of Elm Park, while others simply remember him being in charge of the men who worked in the gardens or 'a sort of caretaker'. Certainly Bob Mitchell was a lot more than just a caretaker. One boy summed Bob's role up nicely when he said that he 'seemed to run the place'.

Other members of staff who worked to maintain the gardens and grounds or on the farm included James McElhinney who for some reason was called 'Cheese' by the boys. He may have earned this name from his work in the dairy. He lived in the east gatelodge. Jimmy Knipe like Bob Mitchell was an invaluable asset as far as mechanical aspects of the farm and yard were concerned: he also worked in the gardens. In the early Thirties the other gardeners included Thomas Kerr, described as head gardener, John Rocks and Willy Bleakley. Mr Kerr lived in the gatelodge on the Knappagh road. Mr Bleakley had worked as a junior groom for the Blacker-Douglas family prior to the school opening in 1921 and retired in 1954 when the school finally closed.

The east gatelodge which was home to James McElhinney for many years. *Courtesy J.A.K. Dean.*

AFTER ELM PARK

WHAT BECAME OF THE BOYS WHEN THEY LEFT ELM PARK? How much their subsequent careers may have depended on their days at Elm Park would be impossible to determine. However a glance at their immediate academic destinations would be very useful, as would a general summary of the type of careers they subsequently followed.

The choice of public schools such as Sedbergh and Shrewsbury might have been influenced by the ease with which they could be reached from connecting ports. We might expect the public schools that Weaving and Seth-Smith attended, Abingdon and Malvern, to be represented among the boys' destinations but about nine boys attended Malvern and none are recorded as going to Abingdon School.

Public School	No. of boys attending
Campbell College	58
St. Columba's	32
Radley	16
Sedbergh	16
Stowe	15
Wellington	13

Table illustrating the top six most popular schools attended by Elm Park boys.

This table accounts for almost 60% of the 288 Elm Park boys and of this group more than half attended either Campbell College in Belfast or St. Columba's College outside Dublin. So quite a proportion of boys continued their education in Ireland.

For the areas of employment followed by the boys themselves and their fathers, see Appendices 5 and 6.

The best-known Elm Park old boy was Brian Faulkner, later Baron Faulkner of Downpatrick who entered the Northern Ireland Parliament as its youngest ever member in 1949 and became Prime Minister in 1971. He resigned from politics in 1976 and died in a hunting accident the following year.

Although there is no official old Elm Parkian association, indeed it is said the founders did not encourage such an association, there have been several reunion dinners. The first took place on 21 November 1975 when sixty-six attended, then in September 1978 thirty-one journeyed back to Killylea and a memorial to their old headmasters was dedicated. Sixty-three joined together in May 1995 for a reunion dinner and in May 2001 fifty-five former pupils attended.

Some of those who attended the dedication service of the memorials in St Mark's Church Killylea, for Hugh Eric Seth-Smith and Willoughby Weaving on 24 September 1978.
Back row: Michael Williams, Robin Charley, Harry Stevenson, John Kinnaird, David Kingan, Peter Acheson, Donn McConnell, Pat Montgomery, Simon Haselden, Tim Herdman.
Middle row: [?], Rev Ian McDonald, Jim Pringle, Desmond Woods, Rev. John Crooks, John Baxter, Ernie Cooke, Tom Dickson, Micky Magill, [?], David Maxwell, Norman Ferguson, Edward Orr, Philip Orr, Angus McConnell.
Front row: Brice Smyth, Felix Gotto, Chris Gotto, Rev. J.R.B. McDonald, Willie Carson, Barney Cowdy.

Service of dedication of memorial in St. Mark's Church Killylea, 24 September 1978.
Left to right: Rev. J.R.B. Mc Donnell, Rev. R.S. Stewart, Rev. J.H. McDonald, Dean J.R.M. Crooks.

CHRONOLOGICAL SUMMARY

It must be asked then: why did Elm Park grow, flourish and decline? Elm Park did not exist in a vacuum. It existed because there was a need for it and as demand fluctuated the school adapted with the times. Elm Park sent fourteen-year-old boys mainly to Irish schools but also to English public schools. As long as the prep school system was the sole conduit through which boys passed to the next stage of their education then social and economic fluctuations to a large extent had little impact on its survival. If however an alternate and cheaper route became available then a dangerous rival had arrived. The world of education after the Second World War was one in which cheaper alternatives were attractive propositions. Factors like the decision made by many parents not to pay for their boys to attend a boarding school influenced Elm Park's fate.

When Elm Park Preparatory School opened its doors in September 1921 it began with the modest complement of just four boys, the two masters and a matron, Miss Seymour. Within a few years numbers had grown to seventeen and by 1928 had reached twenty-seven. For the next decade numbers hovered around thirty but jumped to thirty-six in 1937. In its early days Elm Park grew slowly and matured in the mid-1930s. There is evidence that the number of boys at school was limited by the two masters themselves. Recounting the early days of

An early prospectus from the 1920s.

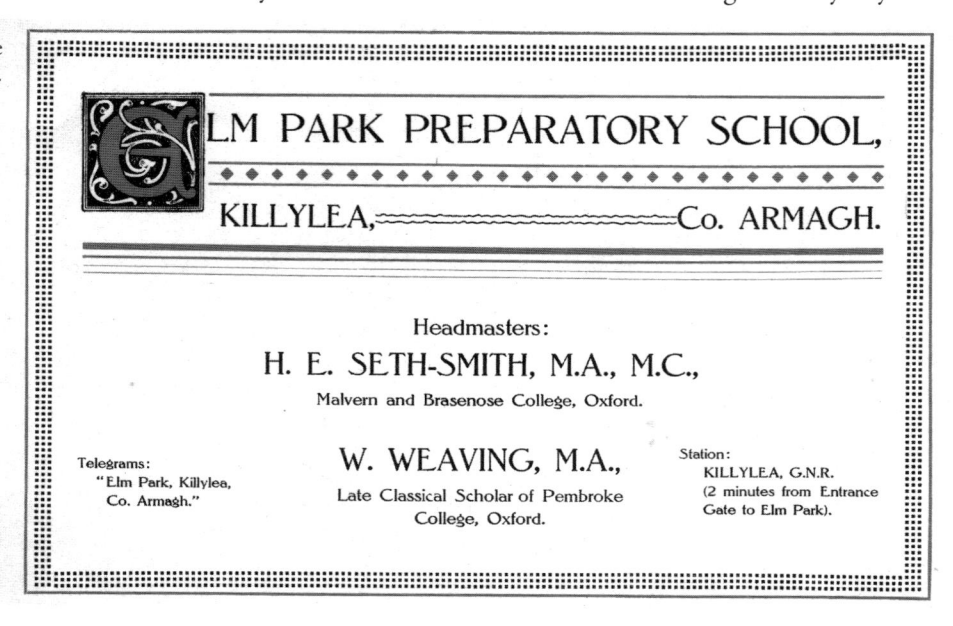

ELM PARK PREPARATORY SCHOOL,

KILLYLEA, —————— Co. ARMAGH.

Headmasters:
H. E. SETH-SMITH, M.A., M.C.,
Malvern and Brasenose College, Oxford.

W. WEAVING, M.A.,
Late Classical Scholar of Pembroke College, Oxford.

Telegrams:
"Elm Park, Killylea, Co. Armagh."

Station:
KILLYLEA, G.N.R.
(2 minutes from Entrance Gate to Elm Park).

This part of the building was converted to classrooms c.1939.

the school Seth-Smith once said that he reckoned the ideal number of boys was around thirty and that allowed Mr Weaving and himself to be choosy when selecting applicants for admission. This also supports the notion that the career of headmaster was actually more of a vocation for the two men who were probably of independent means. They were not depending on revenue from a large influx of new faces each term and could afford to be selective. Seth-Smith had income from a family interest in England and it was said that if a term was particularly poor financially Seth-Smith would ensure the bank balance started off in the black the next term by simply writing a personal cheque.

The jump in the school population at the end of the Thirties was accelerated with the onset of war. Boys whose parents would have normally sent them to English prep schools now found Elm Park a safer and more economical destination. The risks from crossing the U-boat infested Irish Sea or the prospect of boarding close to areas devastated by the Blitz in England were too great and the numbers at Elm Park soared. Added to this must have been other boys who would normally have gone to prep schools in and around the increasingly dangerous Belfast area.

The best gauge for school population, the annual school photographs, are unfortunately non-existent during the war but the number of new boys coming to school each year can be determined from the register and the school population virtually doubled in a year or two. How did the school cope with this influx? The staff sacrificed some of their comforts to ensure more room was made available for the influx of new boarders. During this time a few new dormitories were created to cope with the population boom and Mortimer's Cross was one of them. It slept six boys but before the war it had been Seth-Smith's bedroom. At this time some fine new classrooms were also created in the wing that ran at right angles to the south side of the house.

The war was a watershed in many ways for the school. One small but significant break with the past came when the stiff and staid Eton collars were abandoned in the 1940s. Wartime hardships were no doubt a factor here. Throughout the history of the school the uniform remained more or less the same but it is noticeable from a glance through the annual photos that there were slow subtle changes happening. By 1950 the boys seem much less constrained and more relaxed compared to their predecessors of a few decades earlier.

Of course the major change that happened at this time was the death of Mr Seth-Smith on the last night (19 December) of the winter term 1946. The suddenness of this loss was a severe blow to all concerned: he had been the administrator and solid public face of the school since its inception twenty-five years earlier. The pressure of running the school during the war combined with his duties in the local Home Guard must have taken their toll on Seth-Smith's health. Although Mr Weaving was joint headmaster and partner in the school, his personality was more at home with a classroom of eagerly listening boys than with administrating or talking to parents.

During the latter days of the school Mr Weaving who had always been a retiring man became more withdrawn and the impression given is that some of the other staff simply did their own thing and were beyond his control.

The local Rector from Killylea, Rev. Crooks, helped enormously after the death of Mr Seth-Smith and before the arrival of Mr Williams and to a large extent his role ensured the continuation of the school after the shake up caused by Seth-Smith's death. As well as coaching hockey he also taught Latin, Greek and Scripture.

In September 1947 Michael Williams came to Elm Park fresh from the army after the war and brought energy to the school. He had been a master at Brackenber House School. (See Appendix 3 by Robin Charley.) He was born in 1918, the fourth of five children of R.V. Williams and Margaret (née Pollock). He was educated at Rockport Preparatory School and Wreckin before attending Trinity College Dublin. He served with the Royal Inniskilling Fusiliers during the Second World War. In 1947 he became a partner in Elm Park Limited with Montague Weaving and Willoughby Weaving. In 1951 he married Miss Molly Shea, the matron at Elm Park. When the school closed in 1954 most of the pupils went with Mr Williams and his wife to Rockport. Before the First World War Mr Williams' father had known both Seth-Smith and Weaving when they taught at Rockport. R.V. Williams wrote poetry under the name Richard Rowley and had a special rapport with Weaving. The two writers would exchange their latest works as they were published and corresponded for years.

After Seth-Smith's death some of the outlying farmland was auctioned off and the Seth-Smith family leased the school premises and immediate grounds to the school. Elm Park Limited was set up with three directors, Monty and Willoughby Weaving and Michael Williams. The first term Elm Park opened its doors as a wholly commercial concern was September 1947; the number of boys was thirty-five. Things apparently were looking positive and the following spring mains electricity supply came to the school and so the old generator that had served for so long was no longer needed.

Meanwhile other staff changes soon followed, perhaps initiated by the uncertainty following Seth-Smith's death. In the spring of 1948 Mrs Fleming and her sister Miss Megaw, the matron, left the school. The new matron, Miss Shea, and a replacement for Mrs Fleming, Miss Brownell came in the summer term that year. Another familiar face, Robin Allport who had been a master from 1945, left at the end of the summer term and was replaced by Mr Harris. Miss Brownell was replaced by Miss Parkinson but by Easter term 1949 she too had left. Miss ffrench-Eager arrived in her place but she lasted just one term and was succeeded by Miss Emerson. This lady, it appears, had some radical ideas not usually found in a prep school teacher and would emphasise to the boys in her class the importance of sticking the stamps on their letters upside down to show their contempt for the monarchy.

Mr Harris also left the staff at the end of the summer term 1949 and was replaced the following September by Mr Brian Hanbury. Easter term 1950 saw Miss Nesbitt succeed Miss Emerson. It was during the spring of this year too that Mr Weaving's brother Montague who had joined the staff in 1947 died. His replacement was Mr David Hannon, and by the start of winter term 1950 Mr George Lowdell had succeeded Mr Hanbury. The same term saw Miss McQuaid who came from Omagh taking the place of Miss Nesbitt. In January 1951 Mr Williams and Miss Molly Shea, the matron, were married. During October 1950 Mr Norman Nichols joined the staff coming straight from Trinity College Dublin and as he admitted himself 'knowing next to nothing about teaching'. When he left he was replaced

Headmaster, Mr Michael Williams and his wife Molly Shea the school matron.

Left to right: Peter Acheson, Roger Austin, Miss Nesbitt, Alastair Perceval-Maxwell, Tony Wilkinson. Taken in the summer of 1950.

by Mr G.R. Vaughan who after a short period also left and was ordained into the Church of Ireland. Mr Breeze succeeded him.

Another young man, Trevor Cox, spent a few terms teaching at the school around the same time. His wife Jane Cox was also employed, doing bookkeeping and other administrative tasks. The sad impressions made on him of a once flourishing institution struggling through hard times provided material that he used later when writing under the pen name William Trevor in the book *Old School Ties*. While everyone who witnessed the final years of Elm Park School might not recognise the fine points in Trevor's writing, he nevertheless captured something of the essence of the place, especially of the elderly Mr Weaving. He wrote of him 'He was the only adult I have ever met who understood children perfectly'.

This continual and rapid turnover of staff may have provided the boys with a line of colourful characters to reminisce about years later as well as some excellent teachers. However, the falling numbers and more difficult post-war environment combined with the new profit-driven ethos of Elm Park Ltd to make it increasingly hard to attract quality teachers who were prepared to stay longer than a few terms. The partners were finding things quite difficult and Mr Weaving may have been contemplating his retirement. At the end of 1949 he wrote a letter responding to an advertisement in the *Belfast News Letter* where he stated that: 'We are at present looking for a master with a possible view to his taking over later the place of one of the partners'. Perhaps, though, he was thinking of his brother who was seriously ill at this time and died the following March. Towards the end of summer term 1950 Willoughby himself became

Mr Brian Hanbury taught at Elm Park for a short period in the winter of 1950.

quite ill. He was always frail but made a good recovery during the holidays. He retired in 1953 and left Elm Park to live with his sister in his home town of Abingdon. If the death of Mr Seth-Smith had removed the dynamic force behind the school, the retirement of Mr Weaving removed the embodiment of the vision the originators had conceived in 1921. In a way he was the spirit of the place.

Elm Park finally closed its doors at the end of Easter term 1954: there was no summer term that year. It had been decided that it was not a viable proposition to continue the school in the face of falling numbers. The fact their existing lease was up at that time too, decided the matter. Some of the boys started the new term at Mourne Grange near Kilkeel and a few went to Brackenber House in Belfast. However, the summer term began for the majority of boys, Mr Williams and his wife at Rockport School, back at the institution where forty-two years earlier in 1912 Willoughby Weaving and Eric Seth-Smith had met as young masters.

Most of the school sports trophies went to Rockport School and items like the desks were sold at auction. The school organ which had served for so long accompanying hymns on Sunday evenings was sold to a Presbyterian congregation near the shores of Lough Neagh. The personal possessions of Mr Seth-Smith which still remained at Elm Park were removed back to England by members of his family.

ELM PARK TODAY

Elm park school closed fifty years ago and the house has remained unoccupied since then. Despite the years of abandonment the Speers family who bought the property after the closure of the school have not let the old residence fall into a ruinous state. The roof is intact and most of the windows still retain their glass. The conservatory has been removed but the improvements made in the 1880s are still evident in the dining room ceiling with its elaborate plasterwork. For safety reasons the Speers family can no longer allow access without specific permission being given.

This recent photograph shows the decorated plasterwork of the dining room ceiling, which dates from the 1880s, still very much intact.
Courtesy Andrew Steven.

APPENDICES

1. Register of Elm Park School
2. Old Elm Parkians with connections to the linen industry
3. Family trees of the Maxwell, Close and Blacker families
4. Military careers of Elm Park Headmasters
5. Careers of ex-pupils
6. Occupations of fathers
7. Addresses of fathers
8. School numbers from annual photographs

Elm Park House, although unoccupied for fifty years is in surprisingly good condition as can be seen from this photograph taken recently. *Courtesy Andrew Steven.*

Franklin Cardy and Martin Proctor on the terrace in the 1940s.

APPENDIX 1
REGISTER OF ELM PARK SCHOOL

Introduction

This register would have been impossible to compile if an important document containing most of the data outlined below had not survived. During the lifetime of the school this 1921 diary was used by the headmasters as a notebook to record each boy's details as they entered Elm Park for the first time. It is from it that the boys' names, dates of birth and the year they left school have been taken. It also recorded the public school the parents of the boy intended their son to attend eventually and in the majority of cases this register relies on the notebook for that information too. However, in several cases other sources helped confirm or deny the data in the notebook. The result makes no claim to be a complete record of every boy who attended Elm Park but a substantial amount of effort from John Cowdy and Robin Charley was indispensable in making it as comprehensive a record as practically possible. Some educated guesswork was involved, especially regarding the year boys left school. Finally, the prep schools that the boys who left Elm Park at its closure in 1954 went on to attend are recorded too.

REGISTER OF ELM PARK SCHOOL

		Known as	Date of birth	Left School	Public School
Pupils who first attended in 1921					
Allman	Claude Travers		05 September 1908	1921	St. Columba's
Carson	William Gifford	Willie	22 September 1910	1924	Sedbergh
Wylie	James Owen	Owen	21 January 1910	1924	Sedbergh
Wylie	John Beatty	John	16 February 1912	1925	Sedbergh
Pupils who first attended in 1922					
Davidson	Arthur Lennox Murray		25 July 1912	1924	Campbell College
Dorman Dr	Eric Steen	Eric	30 January 1913	1925	Portora
Gotto	Christopher Corry	Chris	12 December 1911	1925	Dauntsey's
Gotto	Felix Corry	Felix	13 March 1913	1925	Dauntsey's
Greeves	Edmund Owden	Edmund	05 June 1910	1924	Campbell College
Kelly	Bruce	Bruce	15 May 1909	1923	Campbell College
Nasmyth-Miller	Francis John		23 October 1909	1923	Not Recorded
Pears Rev.	John Barbour	John	30 August 1910	1924	Radley
Robb	James Eric E.	Eric	30 July 1912	1926	Wrekin College
Smyth	William Brice	Brice	09 February 1913	1926	Wrekin College
Steen	James Barnet		20 November 1910	1925	St. Bees
Stevenson	George Dougan	George	11 May 1914	1928	Sedbergh
Pupils who first attended in 1923					
Dickie	John Henry Christian	John	04 June 1913	1927	Malvern
Roe	Richard Charles		09 January 1912	1926	St. Columba's
Rogers	John Kave		09 May 1914	1928	Sedbergh
Ross	Vivian Dermot Kennith Conway Conway		20 August 1914	1928	Radley
Pupils who first attended in 1924					
Clark	Leslie Lane	Leslie	10 January 1914	1928	Campbell College
Gotto	Arthur Brian	Brian	26 April 1916	1924	unknown
Mann	Fredrick Alfred William	Fred	02 February 1915	1928	Campbell College
Rentoul Killed in action 25/6/1944, Italy	Lawrence Moore		07 December 1915	1928	unknown
Stewart Rev.	Robert Stevenson	Bob	13 October 1915	1928	unknown
Workman	Robert Little	Roy	30 October 1914	1928	Sedbergh

REGISTER OF ELM PARK SCHOOL

		Known as	Date of birth	Left School	Public School
Pupils who first attended in 1925					
Adair Dr	Thomas M.	Tom	19 September 1916	1929	Campbell College
Beatty	Charles Christopher	Charlie	14 May 1918	1929	Campbell College
Carey	Geoffrey Cyril Raymond	Geoffrey	30 November 1915	1929	Radley
Walsh	Robert Fredrick	Robert	30 January 1916	1929	Marlborough
Williams	Robert Dermot Macmahon	Dermot	26 December 1916	1930	Campbell College
Pupils who first attended in 1926					
Faris	Romney Bowen	Romney	05 September 1916	1930	Malvern
Henderson	Andrew S.	Seamus	06 March 1919	1933	Sedbergh
Henderson	Stanley	Stanley	08 March 1918	1932	Sedbergh
Lytle	Joseph Hannay	Joe	16 August 1917	1931	Campbell College
Millar	John Harold Dundee	Harold	29 May 1917	1931	Campbell College
Scott	Robert Irwin Maddin	Bobby	29 January 1919	1932	Wellington
Stephens	Frank Corry	Corry	13 November 1918	1932	Merchiston
Thompson Killed in action 14/12/1941, Malaya	Humphry Barron		25 January 1916	1929	Campbell College
Woods Lt Col. MC (& Bar)	Adam Desmond	Desmond	14 June 1917	1931	Sedbergh
Pupils who first attended in 1927					
Bulloch	Anthony Alexander	Tony	25 August 1916	1930	Malvern
Dorman	Edward Stephen Patrick		22 November 1915	1929	Malvern
Ewart Sir Ivan Ewart Bt, DSC, JP	William Ivan Cecil	Ivan	18 July 1919	1928	Winchester
Hurst Killed in action 13/11/1940 RNVR, Egypt	William John	Billy	04 June 1918	1932	Campbell College
McDonald Rev.	John Richard Burleigh	Dick	07 May 1917	1931	Campbell College
McKenzie	Kenneth William	Kenneth	08 June 1916	1928	unknown
Millar	Alan McMullan	Alan	28 May 1918	1932	Campbell College
Preston	John Chevallier Wells	John	21 December 1919	1928	unknown
Taggart	Mervyn Alexander	Mervyn	07 March 1918	1928	Sedbergh
Yarr	Robert Lawton	Rab	13 September 1919	1930	Merchiston
Pupils who first attended in 1928					
Boyle	Hugh Charters	Hugh	17 November 1915	1929	Sherborne
Cowdy	Theodore Alfred	Theo	27 January 1919	1933	Sedbergh
Fitzgerald	Anthony John Edward		20 January 1917	1929	Royal Naval College Dartmouth
Millar	Samuel Hampton	Sam	06 June 1919	1933	Campbell College
Woods Killed in action 14/10/1944 Arnhem	Reginald Bryan	Bryan	25 June 1919	1933	Sedbergh

103

ELM PARK: COUNTRY HOUSE TO PREPARATORY SCHOOL

		Known as	Date of birth	Left School	Public School
Pupils who first attended in 1929					
Boyle	John Bruce Armstrong	Bruce	16 November 1919	1930	unknown
Cowdy	William Bryan	Barney	28 May 1920	1934	Sedbergh
Horsbrugh	Patrick B.	Patrick	21 June 1920	1934	Canford
Lytle	George Gerald		31 March 1919	1933	Campbell College
Magill MBE	Robert Henry	Mickey	12 February 1921	1933	Trent College
McMurray	Arthur William		28 April 1920	1929	Not Recorded
Millar	Kenneth Lindsay	Kenneth	11 November 1920	1934	Campbell College
Smyth	Edmund Fitzgerald	Teddy	24 March 1919	1933	Malvern
Stewart	John Hector Noel	Noel	25 December 1919	1933	Royal Naval College Dartmouth
Pupils who first attended in 1930					
Carson	John Martin	John	18 January 1921	1935	Not Recorded
Cooke	Ernest Nikolai	Ernie	20 April 1920	1934	Malvern
Gore-Booth Sir Angus Gore-Booth Bt	Angus J.	Angus	25 June 1920	1934	Radley
McDonald	William Ivan Orr	Billy	23 December 1919	1933	Campbell College
Medlock	Arthur Charles Stevenson	Arthur	03 August 1921	1935	Fettes
Ward FIGRS	Cyril Gordon	Cyril	14 April 1922	1936	St. Columba's
Pupils who first attended in 1931					
Dickson Captain	Thomas Alexander	Tom	09 December 1921	1935	Uppingham
Dougan Dr, JP	George	George	12 July 1920	1934	Campbell College
Haughton Captain, killed in air crash Jan 1953	Thomas Gillmor Wilson	Tommy	07 January 1922	1936	Malvern
Hill	James McLeavy	James	16 November 1921	1935	Malvern
Hill Dr.	Jonathan John McLeavy	Johnny	30 May 1924	1938	Campbell College
Hurst OBE, DL	Charles Talbot	Toby	08 April 1922	1935	Campbell College
Plunkett	Louis LePan	Louis	12 October 1921	1935	Aldenham
Pupils who first attended in 1932					
Adeley	Peter William Brydon	Peter	28 November 1922	1936	Radley
Duffin	Adam Brian	Brian	14 January 1923	1937	Shrewsbury
Good	Horace William	Horace	21 May 1922	1935	Campbell College
Good Rev.	Robert Stanley	Stanley	22 March 1924	1937	Campbell College

REGISTER OF ELM PARK SCHOOL

		Known as	*Date of birth*	*Left School*	*Public School*
Morton Col., MBE, TD	Robert Bruce	Robin	08 June 1922	1936	Wrekin College
Scott	Brian Lockhart	Brian	07 October 1922	1936	Campbell College
Stewart	Charles Fullerton	Charlie	25 September 1922	1937	St. Columba's
Thompson	William Desmond	Desmond	12 July 1923	1935	Campbell College
Woods	Robet Dennis	Dennis	22 July 1923	1937	Sedbergh

Pupils who first attended in 1933

Charley Col., OBE, JP, DL	William Robert Hunter	Robin	25 April 1924	1938	Cheltenham
Dickson DL	William Stephen	Stephen	25 January 1925	1938	Uppingham
Faulkner Lord Faulkner of Downpatrick	Arthur Brian Deane	Brian	18 February 1921	1935	St. Columba's
McCance Major	Reginald Finlay	Finlay	08 June 1924	1938	Radley
MacLeay	Donald Hervey	Donald	10 July 1924	1938	Loretto
Workman	Ian William	Ian	30 July 1925	1938	Uppingham

Pupils who first attended in 1934

Campbell	Morris Edward Dickson	Morris	21 May 1925	1939	Campbell College / Marlborough
Hardy	David Keith	David	27 June 1924	1938	Sedbergh
Jamison Dr	David George	David	14 June 1924	1938	Radley
Orr MC	Robert Edmund	Eddie	16 August 1923	1937	Malvern

Pupils who first attended in 1935

Butler-Rees	Brian	Brian	24 September 1926	1939	Not Recorded
Cowdy	Fredrick Charles	Charlie	20 July 1925	1938	St. Columba's
Crawford	Hugh Reeves	Hugh	28 April 1924	1938	Portora
Fitzgibbon Killed in action 2/1/1951 Korea	Gerald Maurice	Gerry	25 March 1928	1942	Repton
Henderson	Andrew Victor	Drew	03 November 1926	1940	Radley
Mackie	Michael Frazier	Michael	02 June 1926	1940	Campbell College
Pringle	James Mackenzie	Jim	19 July 1926	1940	Campbell College

Pupils who first attended in 1936

Adeley Major	John Michael	Michael	04 December 1928	1942	Radley
Cowdy	John Robert	John	26 August 1927	1941	Campbell College
Duguid	John H.	Jonny	19 March 1928	1937	Wellington

ELM PARK: COUNTRY HOUSE TO PREPARATORY SCHOOL

		Known as	*Date of birth*	*Left School*	*Public School*
Ferguson CBE, DL	Norman Gerald Dickson	Norman	01 August 1926	1940	Campbell College
Hill	Robert William McLeavy	Robin	02 May 1928	1942	Campbell College
Kinnaird	John Alan Lionel	John	23 December 1927	1941	Winchester
Knox-Browne MBE, JP	Mervyn Harvey	Mervyn	29 May 1927	1940	Glenalmond
Ross	John Barry	Barry	13 August 1926	1940	Campbell College
Smith JP	Ian Alan Knighton	Alan	03 January 1927	1941	St. Columba's
Stevenson MBE	Henry Fredrick Dougan	Harry	14 July 1927	1941	Campbell College
Titterington	James Desmond	Desmond	01 May 1928	1943	unknown
Turner Commodore RN	Richard John Fisher	Richard	17 March 1929	1939	Royal Naval College Dartmouth
Wilson DL	Robert Ian Elliott	Ian	24 August 1927	1941	Campbell College

Pupils who first attended in 1937

Carr	James A	Jimmy	23 July 1927	1941	Campbell College
Carson	John Robert	Robert	12 February 1927	1940	Not Recorded
Fforde	Alexander Grant Patrick	Alexander	19 July 1928	1942	St. Columba's
McCance	John Neill	Neill	08 August 1928	1942	Radley
Proctor	Geoffrey Claude	Claude	18 December 1926	1940	Wellington
Whyte	Victor Hamilton	Victor	13 June 1929	1943	Campbell College

Pupils who first attended in 1938

Archer	John Kane	Kane	16 April 1927	1940	Not Recorded
Blood-Smyth	Charles Henry	Henry	31 July 1927	1941	St. Columba's
Carr	William Derek	Derek	19 July 1929	1943	Campbell College
Duffin	Charles Michael	Michael	15 October 1928	1943	Radley
Forrest	William Adrian John	Adrian	29 May 1929	1942	Wellington
Perceval-Maxwell Cmdr RN	Richard Stephen	Dick	09 November 1930	1941	Royal Naval College Dartmouth
Pringle Sir John Pringle, QC, Hon. Mr Justice	John Kenneth	John	23 June 1929	1943	Campbell College
Twigg	Robert Fredrick	Robert	12 May 1928	1942	Campbell College

Pupils who first attended in 1939

Andrews	John Maynard James	John	26 September 1929	1943	Shrewsbury
Burges	Michael Ynyr	Michael	22 March 1931	1944	Eton
Carson	George Alan	George	06 February 1930	1940	Not Recorded

REGISTER OF ELM PARK SCHOOL

		Known as	Date of birth	Left School	Public School
Clarke	Henry George Donnell	Don	05 April 1931	1945	Not Recorded
Cunningham DL	Samuel Barbour	Sam	07 December 1929	1943	Stowe
Dempster	Peter Martin	Peter	07 May 1930	1942	Stowe
Erskine	John Pakenham	John	29 March 1929	1942	St. Columba's
Fisher	John Dudley Francis	John	16 March 1930	1944	St. Columba's
Graham	Robin Ogilby	Robin	15 July 1929	1942	Eton
Henderson	Lionel Victor Crawford	Lionel	06 February 1930	1943	Campbell College
Herdman	Edward Arthur D	Tim	09 May 1930	1944	Oundle
Hobday	David Edmund	David	09 November 1930	1944	Wellington
Hughes	Jeremy Owen Thomas	Jeremy	09 March 1931	1944	Stowe
McConnell Sir Shean McConnell Bt	Robert Shean	Shean	23 November 1930	1944	Stowe
Mackie	John Kay Pringle	John	25 November 1927	1941	Loretto
Maxwell Cmdr, DL	John David	David	21 June 1929	1942	Royal Naval College Dartmouth
Moore Sir William Moore Bt, TD, DL	William Roger	Bill	17 May 1927	1940	Marlborough
Patterson-Moutray	Terence	Derry	05 March 1930	1943	Wellington
Peel	Edward Robert Ernest	Edward	28 August 1926	1939	Canford
Pooler JP, DL	James Hampden Wolfe	James	28 November 1927	1941	Stowe
Roughton	Geoffrey	Geoffrey	01 August 1929	1940	Not Recorded
Stewart Dr	John Hubert Hall	John	06 August 1929	1943	St. Columba's

Pupils who first attended in 1940

Clark MP	Henry Maitland	Henry	11 April 1929	1942	Shrewsbury
Douglas-Nugent Brigadier	Arthur Rainey	Arthur	10 February 1932	1945	Wellington
Kingan OBE, DL	David Robert Samuel	David	08 July 1928	1942	Stowe
Leader	Henry William	Henry	10 December 1930	1944	Winchester
Lowndes	William Jeremy	Jeremy	23 December 1928	1942	Eton
Miller	Herbert David	David	25 January 1931	1943	Not Recorded
Miller	Richard Dennis William	Richard	14 February 1929	1942	Glenalmond
Murland	Charles Daniel	Charlie	14 April 1931	1944	Glenalmond
Sadlier	Francis Arthur	Frank	12 June 1930	1944	Campbell College
Trustram-Eve The Rt Hon. Lord Silsoe QC	David Malcolm	David	02 May 1930	1941	Winchester
Trustram-Eve Col. The Hon. OBE	Peter N.	Peter	02 May 1930	1941	Winchester

ELM PARK: COUNTRY HOUSE TO PREPARATORY SCHOOL

		Known as	Date of birth	Left School	Public School
Pupils who first attended in 1941					
Acworth Major	Hugh John	Hugh	12 April 1933	1946	Cheltenham
Anderson	Allen W.	Allen	01 December 1930	1944	Shrewsbury
Cunningham	Ronald Glencairn	Roly	04 August 1932	1946	Stowe
Darragh	Patrick William F.	Pat	03 March 1932	1945	Royal Naval College Dartmouth
Dicks Lt Col.	John Howard Valentine	John	25 August 1931	1943	Not Recorded
Doyle	Timothy James	Timothy	27 October 1931	1944	Winchester
Faris	Arthur Brian	Brian	26 July 1931	1945	United Service Windsor
Faris	George William Michael	Michael	25 April 1932	1945	Winchester
Herdman CBE, LVO	John Mark Ambrose	Mark	26 April 1932	1945	St. Edwards
Heyn Lt Cmd RN	Denis Neville Fredrick	Denis	27 August 1931	1945	Royal Naval College Dartmouth
McCrum-Miller Rev.	John William	John	09 July 1933	1943	Campbell College
MacGregor	Robert Malcolm Duffield	Malcolm	21 March 1930	1944	Campbell College
Sadlier Col. OBE, TD	Robert Fredrick	Robin	04 March 1932	1945	Campbell College
Stronge MP, killed IRA 21/1/1981	James Matthew	Jim	21 June 1932	1945	Eton
Thorpe	George Montgomery	Monty	20 September 1930	1944	Campbell College
Walbank	Michael Burke	Michael	14 April 1933	1944	Epsom
Whelan	Ernest David Pratt	Ernie	01 January 1929	1944	Campbell College
Pupils who first attended in 1942					
Crawford	Adair Malcolm A	Malcolm	06 August 1934	1943	Winchester
Crozier Lt Com. RN	Thomas Francis Rawdon	Tom	12 April 1933	1946	Repton
Leslie Col., TD, JP, DL	James Francis	James	19 March 1933	1946	Eton
McRae	Christopher Roderick	Roderick	20 February 1934	1947	unknown
Montgomery	Hugh James	Hugh	03 October 1933	1946	Stowe
Montgomery	Stephan Ross	Stephan	15 January 1931	1944	Glenalmond
Morton	Robert	Robert	15 December 1933	1947	Rugby
Mulholland The Rt Hon. The Lord Dunleath, TD, DL	Charles Edward Henry	Henry	23 June 1933	1946	Eton
Sholto-Cooke	Nicholas F.	Nicholas	21 January 1935	1943	Harrow
Sinton	Thomas Fredrick Maynard	Tim	19 October 1933	1945	Stowe

REGISTER OF ELM PARK SCHOOL

		Known as	Date of birth	Left School	Public School
Smith Col.	Patrick Richard Sinclair	Paddy	02 July 1934	1944	Wellington
Stewart Dr	Charles Hall	Charlie	16 February 1933	1946	St. Columba's
Stuart	James Alexander	Jamie	25 April 1933	1946	Marlborough
Turner	Michael Fisher	Michael	27 October 1931	1945	Shrewsbury
Weir	Hubert Godfrey	Godfrey	09 September 1935	1948	Sedbergh

Pupils who first attended in 1943

Barrett	Robert	Robert	28 March 1935	1945	Marlborough
Bell	Robert Kennedy	Robert	24 October 1936	1948	Fettes
Campbell	Godfrey G.	Garry	28 June 1934	1947	Winchester
Cowdy	Christopher	Christopher	16 May 1933	1947	Fettes
Hinchcliffe	John Hugh Spencer	John	08 August 1933	1944	Winchester
Lindsay	Henry Pooler Patrick		01 November 1933	1946	Not Recorded
Maitland-Titterton Col.	David Henry	David	04 January 1933	1946	Campbell College
Maitland-Titterton	Fredrick Lewis	Lewis	28 May 1931	1945	Campbell College
McConnell JP	James Angus	Angus	18 December 1933	1946	Stowe
Montgomery	Patrick David	Patrick	30 December 1934	1948	Glenalmond
Perceval-Maxwell	Michael Benjamin Edward	Michael	08 September 1933	1943	Royal Naval College Dartmouth
Stewart	Hugh Gerald	Hugh	11 April 1934	1948	St. Columba's
Stitt	William Symmons	William	30 May 1934	1945	Not Recorded
Weir Dr	Donald George	Donald	05 March 1934	1947	Glenalmond

Pupils who first attended in 1944

Cardy	William Franklin Gray	Franklin	14 August 1937	1950	Radley
Darling	Terence Brian Moriarty	Terence	01 October 1934	1948	Wellington
Eaton Killed IRA July 1976	Charles Oliver	Oliver	11 October 1933	1947	Campbell College
Finney	Derek Lindsay	Lindsay	15 October 1935	1949	Radley
McMullan	Peter Henry	Peter	19 July 1935	1948	Stowe
Montgomery	John Alexander	Ion	30 October 1935	1947	Eton
Sadlier	Geoffrey Alan	Geoffrey	25 July 1935	1948	Campbell College
Titterington	John Colin	John	08 April 1936	1949	Glenalmond

ELM PARK: COUNTRY HOUSE TO PREPARATORY SCHOOL

		Known as	Date of birth	Left School	Public School
Pupils who first attended in 1945					
Harris	William Brian	Bill	27 April 1935	1948	Campbell College
Haselden	Michael A.	Michael	18 April 1936	1949	St. Columba's
Proctor	Martin James	Martin	25 November 1935	1949	St. Columba's
Swales	Wandy Haswell	Wandy	27 August 1933	1947	Campbell College
Pupils who first attended in 1946					
Acheson DL	Peter Newton	Peter	21 April 1938	1951	Merchiston
Cunningham Dr	John Ronald L.	John	10 April 1937	1950	unknown
Graham	James Edward Laird	Teddy	18 December 1936	1950	Glenalmond
Haselden JP	Christopher Simon	Simon	28 October 1938	1952	Stowe
Heyn	Carl Richard	Carl	07 August 1935	1948	Radley
Hinchcliffe	Peter Robert M.	Peter	14 September 1937	1950	Radley
Lee	John	John	18 March 1936	1949	Campbell College
McMullan	David Fredrick	David	21 July 1938	1951	Stowe
Orr	Edward Francis W.	Eddie	09 March 1936	1949	St. Columba's
Strachan	David Christopher	David	17 June 1938	1950	Radley
Pupils who first attended in 1947					
Boulton Major	Robert George Nicholson	Bob	14 August 1938	1952	St. Columba's
Burrell	John Baker	John	14 July 1938	1952	St. Columba's
Calvert	David Edward	David	07 January 1942	1948	Not Recorded
French	Dominic James	Dominic	06 October 1935	1948	Wellington
French	Owen Gerard M.	Owen	19 May 1937	1950	St. Columba's
Graham Sir John Graham Bt	John Moodie	John	03 April 1938	1951	Glenalmond
McConnell OBE	William Donn	Donn	30 June 1938	1951	Stowe
Orr	Anthony Perceval Samuel	Tony	20 October 1938	1952	St. Columba's
Perceval-Maxwell	Alastair Patrick	Alastair	18 August 1937	1951	St. Columba's
Taylor	Patrick John	Patrick	16 November 1939	1950	St. Columba's

REGISTER OF ELM PARK SCHOOL

		Known as	Date of birth	Left School	Public School	Prep School
Pupils who first attended in 1948						
Armstrong DL	Henry Napier	Henry	28 February 1936	1949	Winchester	
Armstrong	John F.	John	28 February 1936	1949	Eton	
Arnold	Robert Johnston	Robert	09 June 1937	1951	unknown	
Beatty	George Edward C.	Edward	29 January 1940	1953	St. Columba's	
Gordon	Michael Leslie	Michael	14 August 1939	1951	St. Columba's	
Hillis	James Paul	Paul	06 September 1936	1950	Glenalmond	
Hillis	Robert Graham G.	Robin	08 March 1938	1950	St. Columba's	
Jackson	John William	Bill	10 February 1939	1952	Campbell College	
Montgomery	William Howard Clive	Bill	18 January 1940	1952	Eton	
Mullan	William David	William	03 July 1938	1952	St. Columba's	
Stoupe	Robert Ian	Ian	17 April 1940	1953	Glenalmond	
Swiney	John Hazlett Harris	John	16 June 1939	1953	Wellington	
Pupils who first attended in 1949						
Baxter	John Lawson	John	25 November 1939	1953	Oundle	
Bird	Edward	Edward	30 August 1940	1954	unknown	
Boyne	Michael Dermot Butler	Michael	23 April 1942	1952	Not Recorded	Castle Park
Bruce	John Edwin Forde	John	26 October 1937	1952	Rossall	
Butler	Michael Henry	Michael	30 August 1939	1951	Not Recorded	St. Stephen's, Dublin
Chambre ARICS	John Alan	John	02 November 1939	1953	Portora	
Cowdy Maj., DL	Ralph Edward	Ralph	12 November 1940	1954	Repton	
Fulton	George Ogilive	George	14 August 1940	1953	Coleraine Academical Institution	
Greig	John Beamish	John	01 August 1940	1951	Haileybury	
Orr	Philip Claud	Philip	10 August 1940	1954	St. Columba's	
Wilkinson	Thomas Anthony William	Tony	10 May 1941	1954	St. Columba's	

ELM PARK: COUNTRY HOUSE TO PREPARATORY SCHOOL

		Known as	*Date of birth*	Left School	Public School	Prep School
Pupils who first attended in 1950						
Austin	Roger Giles	Roger	07 October 1937	1951	Campbell College	
Brodie	William Hugh	William	27 August 1941	1954	Campbell College	
Carson	William Alan	Alan	02 October 1941	1954	Wrekin College	Rockport
Caruth	Patrick Davis	Corry	31 August 1942	1954	St. Columba's	Headford
Lee	David Gardiner	David	19 May 1942	1954	Campbell College	
MacKinnon	Michael Bingham	Michael	29 May 1941	1950	Wellington	
Montgomery	David Hugh	David	10 June 1942	1954	Stowe	
Russell	William Edward	Billy	04 November 1941	1953	Oundle	Rockport
Taggart	Jackson Albert	Jackson	13 November 1939	1951	Portora	
Topping	Michael Anthony	Michael	10 September 1938	1953	Cheltenham	Brackenber
Pupils who first attended in 1951						
Acheson	David Michael	Michael	09 June 1943	1954	Merchiston	Rockport
Browne	Michael James P.	Michael	06 October 1942	1954	Campbell College	Rockport
Pupils who first attended in 1952						
Blundell	Bernard	Brian	31 July 1945	1954	Not Recorded	Mourne Grange
Blundell	Fredrick George	Ricky	26 July 1943	1954	Not Recorded	Mourne Grange
Gordon	Brian Malcolm	Brian	19 June 1943	1954	St. Columba's	Rockport
Irwin	John Ingram	John	11 February 1943	1954	Marlborough	Rockport
Stoupe	Colin A.	Colin	08 July 1944	1954	Glenalmond	Rockport
Topping	Andrew	Andrew		1954	Cheltenham	Brackenber
Pupils who first attended in 1953						
Archibald	Richard Gordon	Richard	23 February 1945	1954		Rockport
Fulton	John M.	John	10 May 1943	1954	Coleraine Academical Institution	
McManus	David Alister John	Alister	09 September 1945	1954	St. Columba's	Rockport
Pupils who first attended in 1954						
Baker	David Ian	David	19 June 1945	1954	Wellington	Aravon
Hillis	John Gordon	Gordon	13 August 1944	1954	Not Recorded	Rockport

APPENDIX 2

OLD ELM PARKIANS WITH CONNECTIONS TO THE LINEN INDUSTRY

BY JOHN COWDY

During the life span of Elm Park School the linen (and textile industry) in Northern Ireland was of such great importance it seems appropriate to record the names of the boys whose families were immediately involved in this branch of manufacturing. These boys are shown in Table A. Additionally, many boys while not members of 'linen families' yet had strong connections with the industry through their relatives. They are listed in Table B.

Tables A and B record the names of the textile companies with which boys had connections. The year of school entry is given against each boy's Christian name. No claim is made that the list is complete nor that the additional comments encompass the full extent of Elm Park's linen connections.

OLD ELM PARKIANS WITH CONNECTIONS TO THE LINEN INDUSTRY

Table A

Acheson	Peter Acheson (1946), Michael Acheson (1951)	David Acheson Ltd (Castlecaulfield)
Adair	Tom Adair (1925)	Thomas Adair & Son (Cookstown)
Andrews	John Andrews (1939)	John Andrews & Co. Ltd (Comber)
Beatty	Charlie Beatty (1925), George Beatty (1948)	Coalisland Weaving Co. Ltd (Coalisland)
Campbell	Gary Campbell (1943), Donald H. MacLeay (1933)	Henry Campbell & Co. Ltd (Mossley)
Carr	Jimmy Carr (1937), Derek Carr (1938)	William Liddell & Son Ltd (Donacloney)
Carson	Alan Carson (1950), mother was Boyd, father was Willie Carson (1921)	Blackstaff Flax Spinning and Weaving Co. Ltd (Belfast)
Charley	Robin Charley (1933)	J. & W. Charley & Co. Ltd (Dunmurry)
Clark	L.L. Clark (1924)	John A. Clark & Co. Ltd (Castledawson)
Clark	Henry Clark (1939)	William Clark & Sons Ltd (Upperlands)
Cooke	Ernie Cooke (1930)	John Preston & Co. (Belfast) Ltd
Cowdy	Theo Cowdy (1928), Barney Cowdy (1929), Charlie Cowdy (1935), John Cowdy (1936), Christopher Cowdy (1943), Ralph Cowdy (1949)	Anthony Cowdy & Sons Ltd (Banbridge)
Dickson	Tom Dickson (1931), Stephen Dickson (1933)	Dickson & Co. (Dungannon) Ltd (Dungannon)
Ewart	Ivan Ewart (1927), Brice Smyth (1922)	William Ewart & Son Ltd (Belfast)
Faulkner	Brian Faulkner (1933)	Belfast Collar Co. Ltd (Belfast)
Ferguson	Norman Ferguson (1936)	Thomas Ferguson & Co. Ltd (Banbridge)
Gordon	Michael Gordon (1948), Brian Gordon (1952)	Linen Thread Co. Ltd (Hilden, Lisburn)
Gotto	Chris Gotto (1922), Felix Gotto (1922), Brian Gotto (1924)	Old Bleach Linen Co. Ltd (Randlestown)
Graham	Robin Graham (1939)	York Street Flax Spinning Co. Ltd
Greeves	Edmund Greeves (1922)	Portadown Weaving Co. Ltd (Portadown)
Hardy	David Hardy (1934)	T.L. Hardy & Co. Ltd (Belfast)
Haselden	Simon Haselden (1946)	William Ross & Co. Ltd (Belfast)

CONNECTIONS TO THE LINEN INDUSTRY

Haughton	Tommy Haughton (1931)	Frazer & Haughton Ltd (Cullybackey)
Henderson	Stanley Henderson (1926), Seamus Henderson (1926), Drew Henderson (1935), Lionel Henderson (1939)	Whiteabbey Bleaching Co. Ltd (Whiteabbey)
Herdman	Mark Herdman (1941)	Herdman's Ltd (Sion Mills)
Herdman	Tim Herdman (1939)	Henry Matier & Co. Ltd (Belfast)
Hillis	Robin Hillis (1948), Paul Hillis (1948), Gordon Hillis (1954)	Co. Down Weaving Company Ltd (Belfast)
Hurst	Billy Hurst (1927), Toby Hurst (1931)	Hurst's Ltd (Drumaness)
Kinnaird	John Kinnaird (1936)	Kinnaird Textiles Ltd (Belfast)
McCance	Finlay McCance (1933), Neill McCance (1937)	Kirkpatrick Brothers Ltd (Ballyclare), Kilwee Bleaching Co. Ltd (Dunmurry)
Mackie	Michael Mackie (1935), John Mackie (1939)	James Mackie & Sons Ltd (Belfast)
Medlock	Arthur Medlock (1930)	Murphy & Stevenson Ltd (Dromore)
Mulholland	Henry Mulholland (1942), Robin Graham (1939)	York St Flax Spinning Co. Ltd (Belfast)
Murland	Charlie Murland (1939)	James Murland Ltd (Castlewellan)
Pringle	Jim Pringle (1935), John Pringle (1938)	Hillsborough Linen Co. Ltd (Hillsborough)
Proctor	Claude Proctor (1937), Martin Proctor (1945)	Joseph Orr (Cranagill) Ltd (Benburb)
Rogers	J.K. Rogers (1923)	Clarence Finishing Co. Ltd (Belfast)
Russell	Bill Russell (1950)	Henry's Belfast Ltd (Archibald Russell)
Sinton	Tim Sinton (1942)	Thomas Sinton & Co. Ltd (Tandragee)
Smyth	Brice Smyth (1921), Teddy Smyth (1929)	Smyth's Weaving Co. Ltd (Banbridge)
Stevenson	Harry Stevenson (1936), John Lee (1946), David Lee (1950)	Moygashel/Stevenson & Sons Ltd (Dungannon)
Stoupe	Ian Stoupe (1948), Colin Stoupe (1952)	Hicks Bullock & Co. Ltd (Belfast)
Thomson	Desmond Thomson (1932)	Thomson Dye Works (Drumbeg)
Titterington	Desmond Titterington (1936), John Titterington (1944)	James Titterington & Sons Ltd (Belfast)
Williams	Dermot Williams (1925), Michael Williams (1947-54) [last Headmaster]	McBride & Williams Ltd (Belfast)

ELM PARK: COUNTRY HOUSE TO PREPARATORY SCHOOL

Given below are names of boys who had other strong family connections with the linen trade.

Table B

Anderson	Allen Anderson (1941)	His family were the Andersons in Anderson & McAuley Ltd, the leading Belfast store retailing linen.
Carson	Willie Carson (1921)	His wife was a daughter of Thornton Boyd of the Blackstaff Co. and their son Alan (1950) attended school.
Crawford	Malcolm Crawford (1942)	His mother was an Andrews of John Andrews & Co. Ltd (Comber).
Duffin	Brian Duffin (1932), Michael Duffin (1938)	Grandchildren of Samuel Barbour of the Linen Thread Co. Ltd (Hilden) and their father's family had linen, spinning and weaving interests in the 19th century.
Erskine	John Erskine (1939)	His father was sales director of William Ewart & Son Ltd (Belfast).
Forrest	Adrian Forrest (1938)	His grandfather was Sir William Quartus Ewart former chairman of William Ewart & Son Ltd (Belfast).
McConnell	Shean McConnell (1939), Angus McConnell (1943), Donn McConnell (1947)	Grandchildren of James S. Reade director of York St Flax Spinning Co. Ltd (Belfast) (where brother R.H.S. Reade was chairman).
MacLeay	Donald H. MacLeay (1933)	A connection of the Campbell family Henry Campbell Ltd (Mossley).
Magill	Mickey Magill (1929)	His mother was a daughter of O.B. Graham (Senior) of York St Flax Spinning Co. Ltd (Belfast).
Miller	John McCrum Miller (1941)	Grandmother was a McCrum of McCrum, Watson & Mercer Ltd (Milford).

CONNECTIONS TO THE LINEN INDUSTRY

Pears	John Pears (1922)	His father was Rowland Pears of Fairbairn, Lawson Combe Barbour Ltd (Belfast) the linen etc., machinery manufacturers.
Smith	Alan Knighton Smith (1936), Gerry Fitzgibbon (1935)	Uncle was Noel Smith of John Compton & Co. Ltd (Glenanne).
Stewart	John Stewart (1939), Charlie Stewart (1942)	Their grandfather was W. Hubert Webb chairman Old Bleach Linen Co. Ltd (Randalstown).
Swiney	John Swiney (1948)	Mother was Stevenson of Stevenson & Sons Ltd (Dungannon).
Turner	M.F. Turner (1942)	Father was director of Linen Industry Research Institute (Lambeg).
Williams	Dermot Williams (1925), Michael Williams, last Headmaster	McBride & Williams Ltd (Belfast) was their family firm.
Woods	Desmond Woods (1926), Bryan Woods (1928), Dennis Woods (1932)	They were nephews of Fred Sinton (Thomas Sinton & Co. Ltd, Gilford) and their grandmother was a Upritchard of J. & T. Upritchard, Elmfield.

APPENDIX 3

FAMILY TREES OF THE MAXWELL, CLOSE AND BLACKER FAMILIES

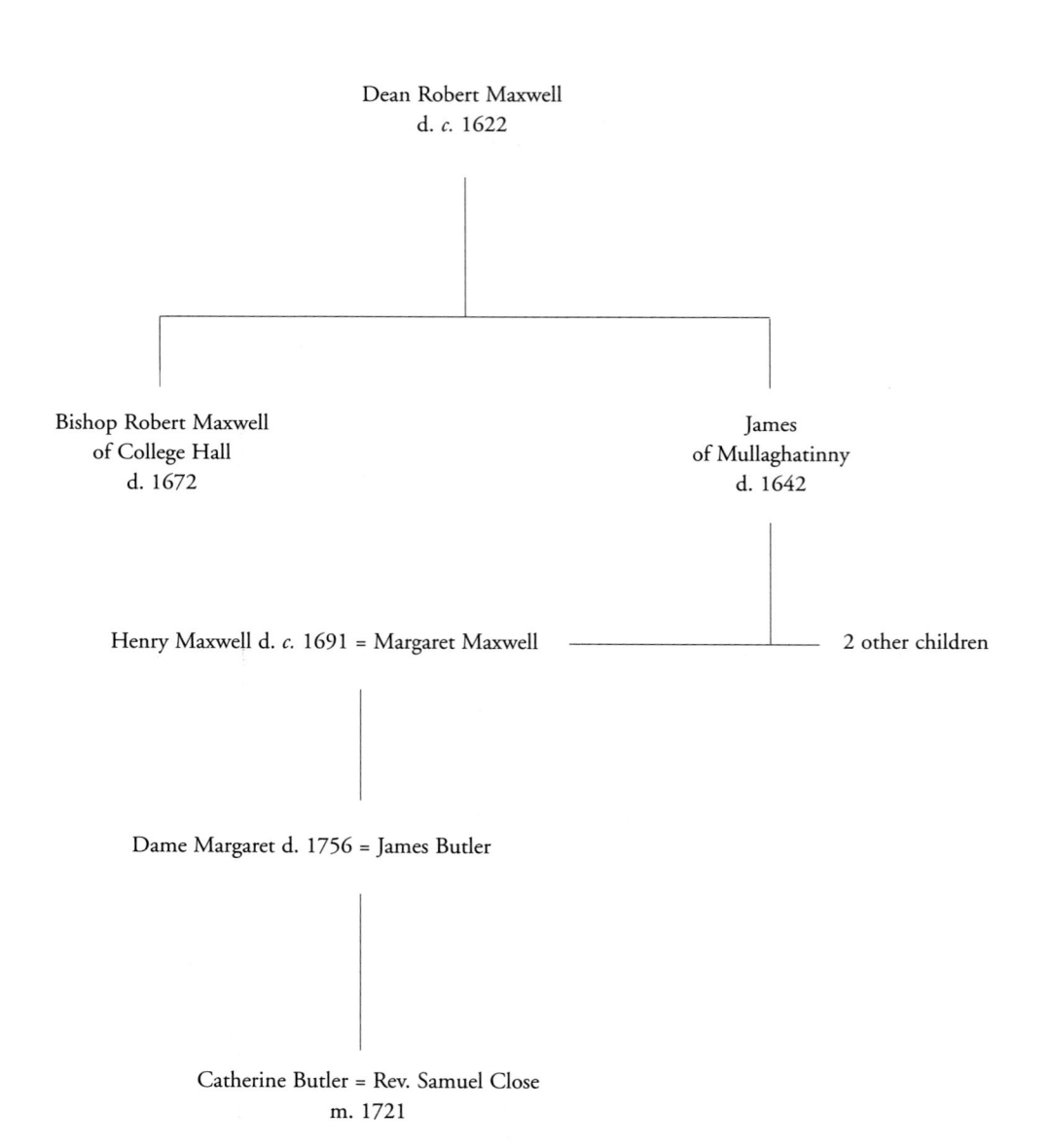

```
                        Dean Robert Maxwell
                            d. c. 1622
                                │
                ┌───────────────┴───────────────┐
      Bishop Robert Maxwell                  James
        of College Hall                  of Mullaghatinny
            d. 1672                          d. 1642
                │                                │
                │                    ┌───────────┴───────────┐
    Henry Maxwell d. c. 1691 = Margaret Maxwell         2 other children
                │
                │
        Dame Margaret d. 1756 = James Butler
                │
                │
          Catherine Butler = Rev. Samuel Close
                    m. 1721
```

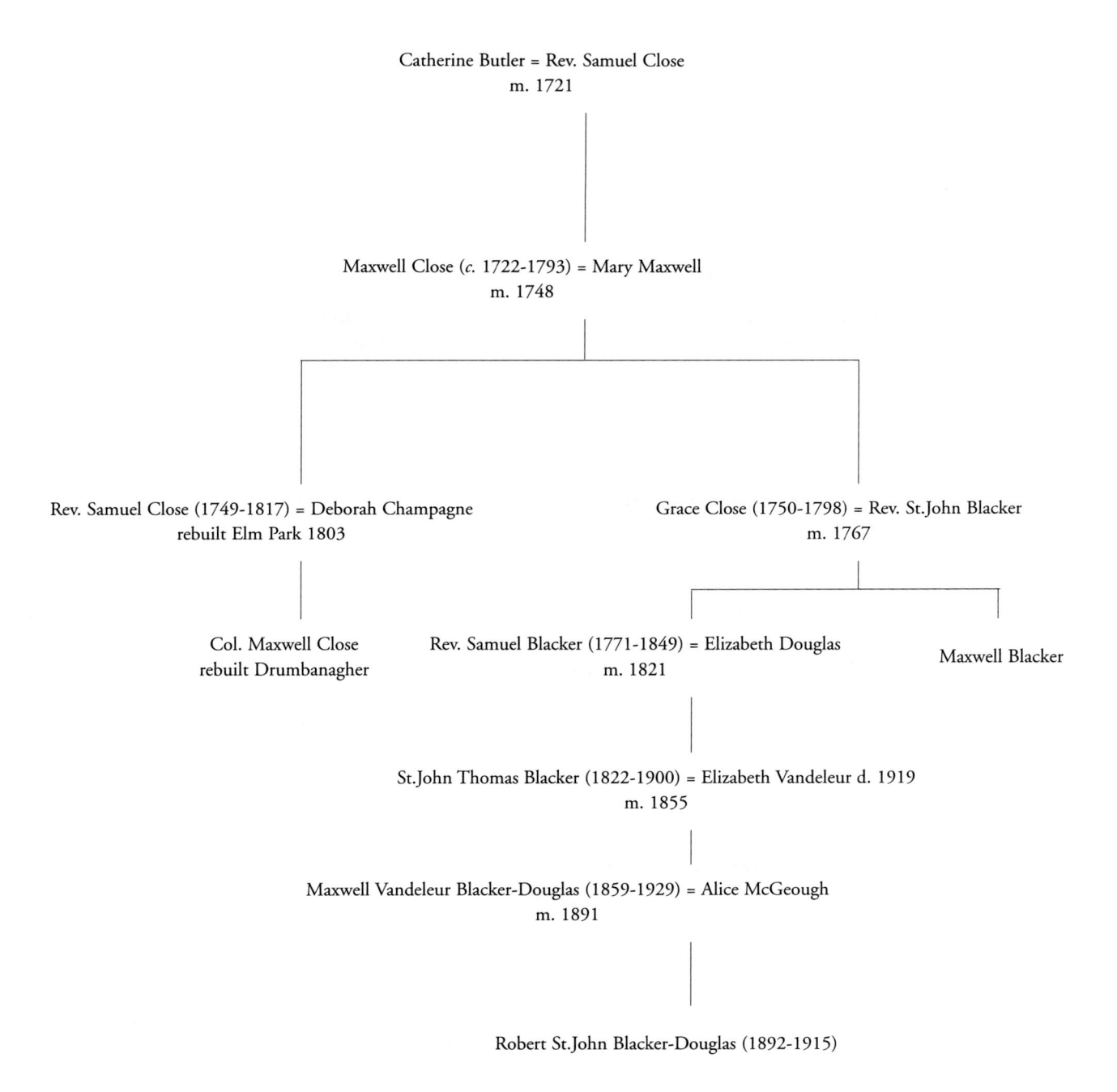

```
                    Catherine Butler = Rev. Samuel Close
                                m. 1721
                                   │
                    Maxwell Close (c. 1722-1793) = Mary Maxwell
                                m. 1748
                    ┌──────────────────┴──────────────────┐
Rev. Samuel Close (1749-1817) = Deborah Champagne    Grace Close (1750-1798) = Rev. St.John Blacker
         rebuilt Elm Park 1803                                m. 1767
                    │                              ┌──────────┴──────────┐
        Col. Maxwell Close          Rev. Samuel Blacker (1771-1849) = Elizabeth Douglas    Maxwell Blacker
        rebuilt Drumbanagher                       m. 1821
                                                      │
                            St.John Thomas Blacker (1822-1900) = Elizabeth Vandeleur d. 1919
                                                m. 1855
                                                      │
                            Maxwell Vandeleur Blacker-Douglas (1859-1929) = Alice McGeough
                                                m. 1891
                                                      │
                                   Robert St.John Blacker-Douglas (1892-1915)
```

119

APPENDIX 4

MILITARY CAREERS OF ELM PARK HEADMASTERS

BY ROBIN CHARLEY

H.E. Seth-Smith
Hugh Eric Seth-Smith was born on 23 November 1887 at St Margaret's Mansions, Victoria Street, Westminster, the son of Charles Edward and Florence Maude née Stevenson. His father was a Barrister at Law. He was educated at Malvern and Oxford where he obtained a BA. He served in the Inns of Court OTC and was a schoolmaster at Rockport Preparatory School, Craigavad, Co. Down.

He applied for a commission on 7 October 1914, expressing a preference for 4th RIR. His permanent address at that time was The Old Rectory, Bletchingley, Surrey, the home of Rev. A.H. De Foutraine, Rector of Bletchingley.

He joined 2nd RIR and was posted to B Coy on 11 July 1915. He was wounded on 9 August 1915, while in charge of a digging party. On 20 August he embarked from Calais for Dover aboard the *SS Dieppe*. GSW right thigh, flesh wound. He wrote to the War Office on 29 August from the Old Rectory, advising that he was attending Dr Abbot's Red Cross Hospital, Bletchingley. A Medical Board at the War Hospital, Croydon on 6 September 1915 reported that his general health was good, but the wound had not yet healed. A Medical Board at the Reception Station, Guildford on 5 October 1915 determined that the wound had healed but the leg muscles were weak.

He reported for light duty to 4th RIR at Carrickfergus on 27 October. On 28 January 1916 he was certified fit for general service. He was appointed Lt on 15 March 1916. On 21 October he embarked from Southampton for Le Havre and joined 7th RIR on 1 November. Leave was granted 16-26 May 1917 and 1-11 October 1917. He was sent to the UK to appear before a board for commissions in the Indian Army on 16 October 1917, as 7th RIR was disbanding and was appointed Staff Capt. 25th Infantry Bde and to be T/Capt.

whilst so employed. He was awarded the MC (*London Gazette*, 1 November 1918). He disembarked at Boulogne with HQ 16th Division on 31 July 1918.

He was granted leave to the UK 31 October to 14 November. On 15 February 1919 he was admitted to No. 24 Field Ambulance and No. 39 Stationary Hospital with a corneal ulcer and transferred to England on 12 March 1919. He was demobilised on 10 April 1919 with an A1 medical rating.

After the war, he and H.W. Weaving toured Northern Ireland on a motorcycle and sidecar searching for a suitable house and estate to start a boys' prep school. In 1921 they founded Elm Park School, Killylea, Co. Armagh, which lasted until 1954 when the remaining boys joined Rockport School. Seth-Smith died in 1946.

H.W. Weaving

Harry Willoughby Weaving was born at Cutteslowe, RSD, Oxford on 6 June 1882. He was the son of Harry Walker and Beatrice Anne née Armitage, Pewit House, Abingdon, Berks. His father was a Brewer and Maltster. He was educated at Abingdon School and at Pembroke College, Oxford, where he obtained a classical MA and was a protégé of Robert Bridges. Owing to illness, he did not start working until he was thirty and became a junior master at Rockport Preparatory School, Craigavad, Co. Down.

He applied for a commission on 7 October 1914, expressing a preference for 4th RIR. He joined 2nd RIR from 4th RIR on 12 July 1915 and was posted to D Coy. He was sent to hospital on 7 September 1915 and was evacuated from Dieppe to Dover on 9 September. The cause of return was 'sickness (heart trouble)', which was his own description. He seemed to have been generally debilitated and probably a neurasthenia case. Robert Bridges, Chilswell, near Oxford, wrote to the War Office on his behalf on 23 October: 'Lt Weaving was invalided home. After one or two months in hospital he had six weeks leave, dating from September 23, which expires November 3. I make myself responsible for the following statements. (1) He should never have been passed as fit for active service. (This is confirmed by result.) (2) If he returns, he will break down again. I speak from personal knowledge (he is a neighbour), and I have a letter from an officer who was out with him in France asking me if I cannot make some statement of his case to the authorities to prevent a mistake. As Lt Weaving's breakdown was heart failure – he fainted in the trenches, and his life was despaired of in hospital – it is possible that, since he seems to be recovering well, he may after some months of absolute rest make a fair show before the Board. Also, he need not be discharged as wholly unfit. He has high mental qualities, and is popular with the men. At least I judge this last to be so from his telling me that his contact with them was the pleasantest experience of all his life – so that it might be possible to transfer him to some home unit where he might instruct recruits – to which, especially after his actual experience of the trenches, he would seem to be particularly fitted. His own feeling is that he does not like the idea of being out of it, but is aware that he will break down and be only a burden if he should be sent out again. He is willing to do anything ... My being a Fellow of the R. College of Physicians may perhaps lend professional weight to my opinion.'

A Medical Board on 3 November determined that he was permanently unfit for general service, and did not consider that his condition had been caused or exacerbated by military service. WO to GOC Irish Command 11 November: he was to be instructed to resign his commission on the grounds of ill health and to be thanked for placing his services at the country's disposal at time of crisis. His resignation was approved on 18 November 1915.

He returned to teaching at Rockport School. After the War, he and H.E. Seth-Smith toured Northern Ireland on a motorcycle and sidecar searching for a suitable house and estate to start a prep school. In 1921 they founded Elm Park School, Killylea, Co. Armagh. He wrote about the Irish and English countryside, and his poetry became very popular. The following is an extract from *Flanders*:

Man has his life of butterflies
In the sunshine of sacrifice, Brief and brilliant, but more
Guerdon than the honey flower And more glory than the grace
Of their gentle floating pace.

He retired in 1953 and died at Abingdon in 1976 aged 94.

M.V.R. Williams
Michael Valentine Rowley Williams was born in Belfast on 8 May 1918, the son of Rowley Valentine Williams and Margaret Sophie (née Pollock) and the fourth of five children – Allan, Joan, Betty, Michael and Barbara. He was educated at Rockport Preparatory School 1927-32, Wreckin College 1932-36 and Trinity College Dublin 1938-40 and 1946 (BA). Before going up to TCD, he taught for a time at Brackenber House School, Belfast.

Michael did not follow his father into the linen, cotton, handkerchief and fancy goods business, where the family had quite a substantial involvement. In 1900 Michael's grandfather and Thomas McBride formed a limited liability company – McBride and Williams Limited – and Michael's father was managing director for a period leading up to the reconstruction of the business in 1933 when he dropped out of active management giving him more time to devote to his writings.

Michael's brother Allan was a boy at Rockport School (1913-17) and his father had met both H.E. Seth-Smith and H.W. Weaving while they were assistant masters at the school before they went off to the War in 1914, Willoughby Weaving having returning there after he was medically discharged and invalided home in November 1915. Mr Williams who published poems under the *nom de plume* 'Richard Rowley' got to know H.W. Weaving well. They exchanged new publications as they appeared. Eleven volumes of the Weaving books have since been presented by Michael Williams to the Armagh County Museum.

In July 1940 Michael left TCD and enlisted as a fusilier with the Royal Inniskilling Fusiliers at 25 ITC Omagh. He soon passed a War Office Selection Board and was sent to 16th Officer Cadet Training Unit at Droitwich in November 1940.

In February 1941 he was commissioned 2nd Lieutenant into the Royal Inniskilling Fusiliers and was posted overseas in June 1941 to join the 1st Battalion in India. After a long and pleasant sea voyage he reported as a 2nd Lieutenant to the 1st Battalion at Wellington in South India in September 1941. In October the battalion was moved to Meerut near Delhi where it stayed until 1942.

The Japanese, with the help of the Siamese, invaded Burma in January 1942. The 'Skins' were sent into action to stem the advance of the Japanese and to prevent them capturing the oilfields at Yenangyaung. As part of the 1st Burma Division the 'Skins' fought with great courage in the First Burma Campaign. They counter-attacked the Japanese at the oilfields in temperatures of 114 degrees fahrenheit. Flames roared from the oil tanks and wells which were all successfully destroyed. The overwhelming numbers of Japanese which they met in the first stage of the Burma campaign meant a grim 500 mile lightning withdrawal with countless ambushes and counterattacks through the most pestilent and malarial country in the world. The long march to the Indian frontier, most of the unit being hopelessly weak with malaria, lasted until late June 1942, only 114 reaching the border, among them Michael who was then evacuated to hospital. It was not until September 1942 that he was able to rejoin the battalion, on promotion to Lieutenant at Jullundur in the Punjab near Lahore to be reinforced, re-equipped and retrained for the next effort, the Second Burma Campaign.

The next month, at the start of the Second Burma Campaign, the battalion moved forward from Comilla on the border to Feni still in Bengal and then towards Chittagong. The Japanese were in strong defensive positions on the Arakan peninsula. Pushing into the Arakan threatened the enemy's flank and their plans to attack India. As part of 47th Indian Infantry Brigade, the 1st Battalion fought through high ridges and trackless jungle against well concealed Japanese machine gun and mortar positions. The Japanese had to redirect vital reinforcements against this threat in the Arakan. When the Brigade, after suffering many casualties, was ordered to withdraw to the coast there were no roads or even mule tracks through the jungle ridges. However, broken up into small detachments of survivors, members of the unit reached Kyaukpandowrma on the northern shore of the Arakan peninsula in April 1943. The unit had gained a tremendous reputation again, but Michael, like many others, was shortly admitted to hospital, as before, with malaria and infective hepatitis.

Temporarily downgraded to medical category B he was posted to the Base Reinforcement Camp at Deolali and promoted to Captain on its staff. Fit again in June 1943 he was posted back as Lieutenant to the 1st Battalion and became Assistant Adjutant and Intelligence Officer. For two years from May 1943 to May 1945 the 1st Battalion remained 'on guard' in India. He was promoted Captain and Adjutant, March 1944 and in September 1945 acting major, commanding D Company.

In December 1945, owing to his father's serious illness he was posted on compassionate repatriation to the UK. January 1946 saw him in the Irish Holding Battalion at Newcastle-under-Lyme as a Captain and then he was posted to the Royal Military College Officer Cadet Unit at RMA, Sandhurst, as a Weapons Training Instructor.

In June 1946 he was demobilised from the Army and returned to complete his Bachelor of Arts degree at TCD. Michael was awarded the following medals: 1939-45 Star, Burma Star, Defence Medal and War Medal. His elder brother Captain J.R.A. Williams served in 51st Battalion, Royal Inniskilling Fusiliers (Home Service Battalion) throughout the War.

After graduating from TCD Michael returned to teaching at Brackenber House School, Belfast 1946-47. In September 1947 he joined the staff at Elm Park, H.E. Seth-Smith having died in 1946. In 1948 he became a partner in Elm Park Limited with H.W. Weaving and his younger brother M.G. Weaving. Montague Weaving died two years later. In the early 1950s, whilst teaching at Elm Park, he served as a volunteer captain as 2nd IC of the Armagh Company of the Royal Irish Fusiliers in the revived Ulster Home Guard.

In 1951 he married Mollie Shea, matron of Elm Park. In 1953 Willoughby Weaving retired and went to live with his sister in Abingdon, Berkshire. In 1954 Elm Park closed and most of the remaining pupils came with Michael and his wife to Rockport Preparatory School, Craigavad in the summer term.

In 1989 he retired from teaching at Rockport School. Sadly his wife Mollie died in 1991.

For many years he was Branch Secretary and Poppy Day Organiser of the Craigavad and Helen's Bay Royal British Legion. He now lives at Helen's Bay.

APPENDIX 5

CAREERS OF EX PUPILS

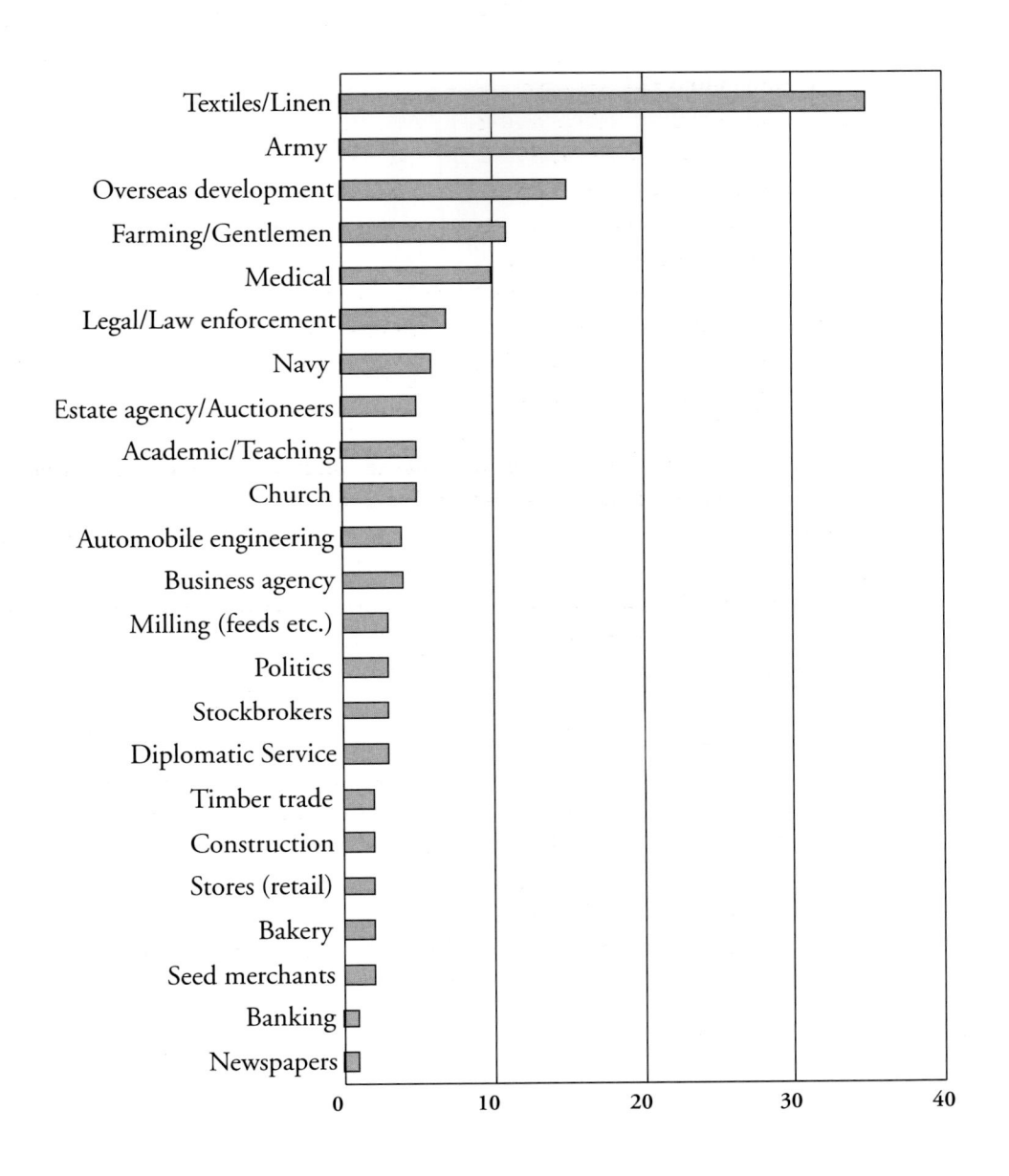

Career	Count
Textiles/Linen	35
Army	20
Overseas development	15
Farming/Gentlemen	11
Medical	10
Legal/Law enforcement	7
Navy	6
Estate agency/Auctioneers	5
Academic/Teaching	5
Church	5
Automobile engineering	4
Business agency	4
Milling (feeds etc.)	3
Politics	3
Stockbrokers	3
Diplomatic Service	3
Timber trade	2
Construction	2
Stores (retail)	2
Bakery	2
Seed merchants	2
Banking	1
Newspapers	1

APPENDIX 6
OCCUPATIONS OF FATHERS

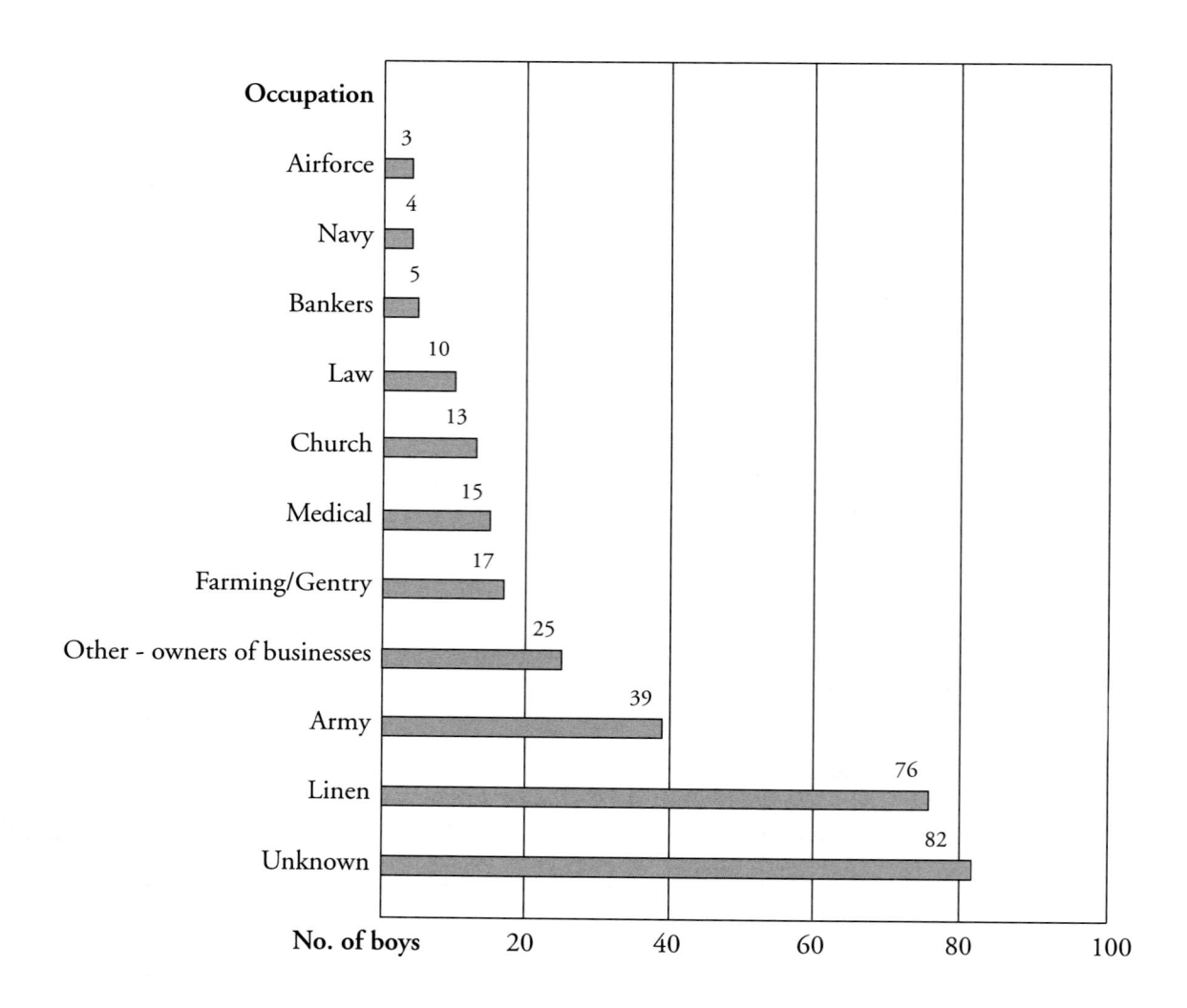

Occupation	No. of boys
Airforce	3
Navy	4
Bankers	5
Law	10
Church	13
Medical	15
Farming/Gentry	17
Other - owners of businesses	25
Army	39
Linen	76
Unknown	82

APPENDIX 7
ADDRESSES OF FATHERS

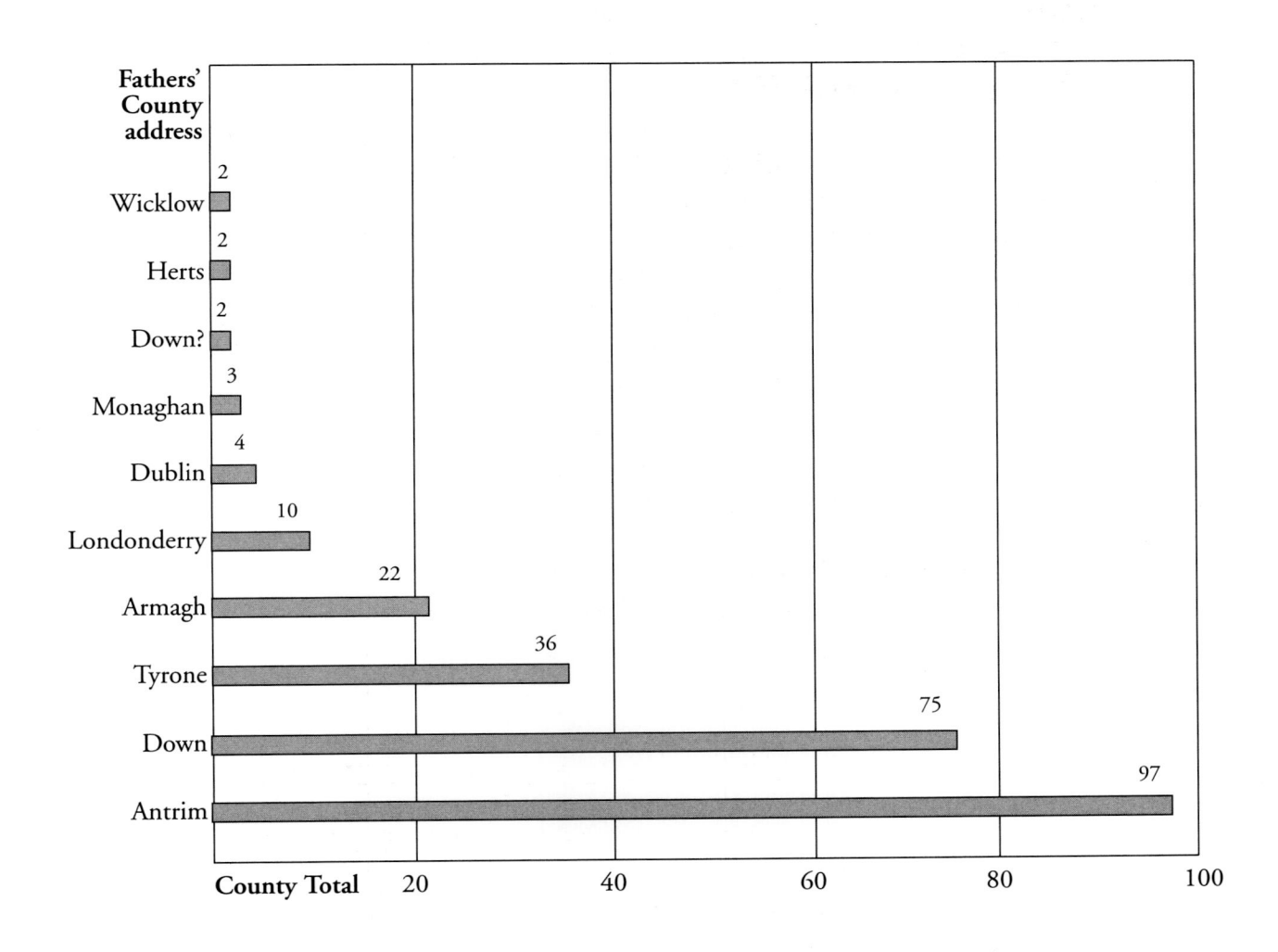

Fathers' County address	County Total
Wicklow	2
Herts	2
Down?	2
Monaghan	3
Dublin	4
Londonderry	10
Armagh	22
Tyrone	36
Down	75
Antrim	97

APPENDIX 8

SCHOOL NUMBERS FROM ANNUAL PHOTOGRAPHS

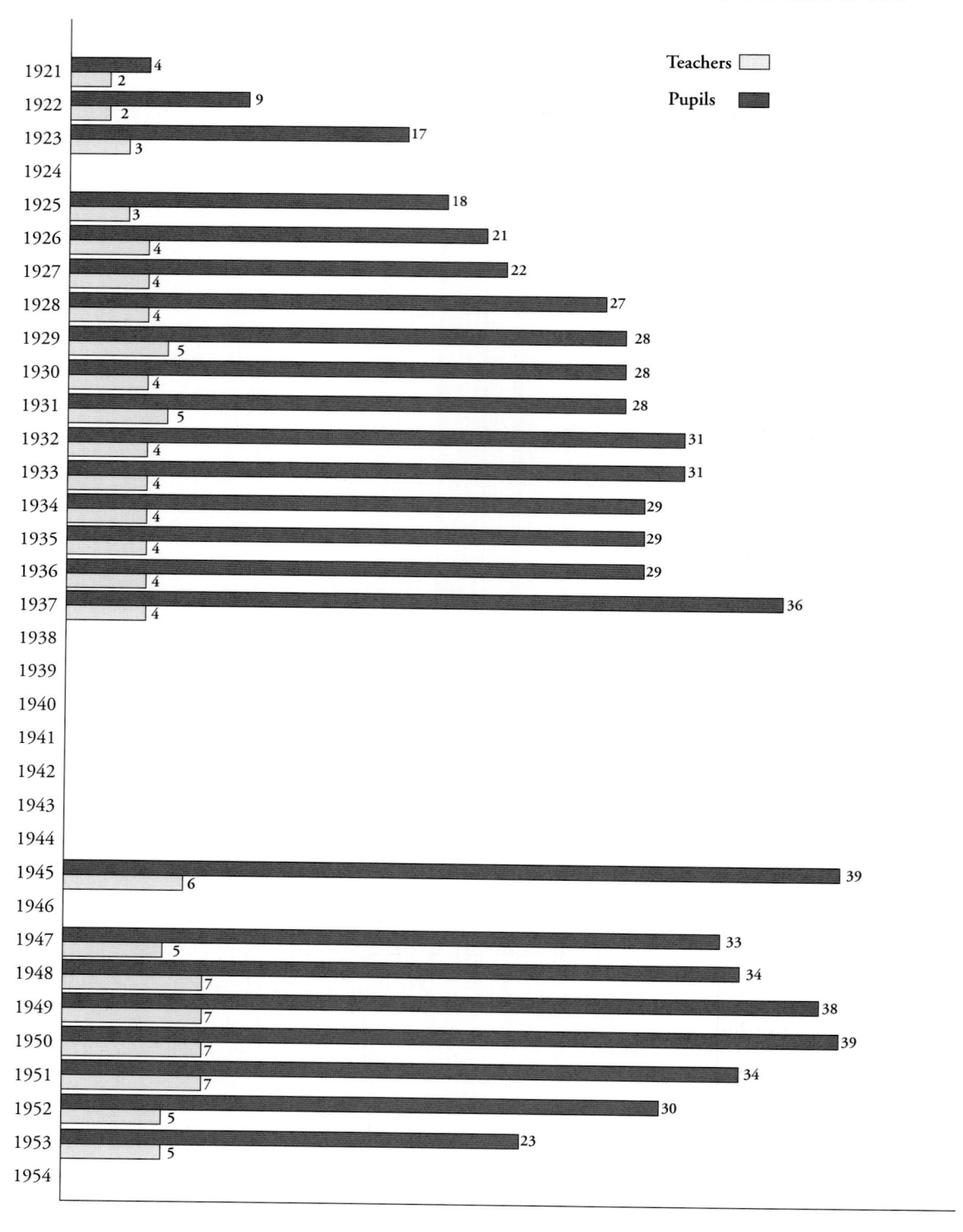

Year	Teachers	Pupils
1921	2	4
1922	2	9
1923	3	17
1924		
1925	3	18
1926	4	21
1927	4	22
1928	4	27
1929	5	28
1930	4	28
1931	5	28
1932	4	31
1933	4	31
1934	4	29
1935	4	29
1936	4	29
1937	4	36
1938		
1939		
1940		
1941		
1942		
1943		
1944		
1945	6	39
1946		
1947	5	33
1948	7	34
1949	7	38
1950	7	39
1951	7	34
1952	5	30
1953	5	23
1954		

BIBLIOGRAPHY

UNPUBLISHED SOURCES

PRO, London

Wills of members of Close and Blacker families, prob. 11/1597; prob. 11/2157; prob. 11/2092.

Armagh County Museum

Dr. William Lodge Kidd's case book, Accession No. 153-1960.

Paterson, T.G.F., Armachiana, miscellaneous historical notes on Co. Armagh, vols. 2, 9, 10, 25.

1641 Depositions, typescript copy by T.G.F. Paterson.

Close family tree, Paterson ms 23B.

Armagh See rentals, typescript copy by T.G.F. Paterson.

Paterson ms collection held in Armagh County Museum, No. 23, 63, 159, 239.

Damp press letter books from Boyle estate office, Accession No. 168-1962.

A view of the archbishopric of Armagh by Thomas Ashe, 1703, [Photostat].

Irish & Local Studies library, Armagh

Census of Ireland 1901. County of Armagh, Poor Law Union of Armagh, District Electoral Division – Ballymartrim, Townland of Mullaghatinny or Elm Park, Form A & B1, Microfilm Reel 6.

Public Record Office of Northern Ireland

Townland valuation field book, 1836, Barony of Armagh, Parish of Tynan, VAL/12B/10/10/A, p. 60.

PUBLISHED SOURCES

Alexander, Eleanor, Jane (ed.), *William Alexander, Primate Alexander, Archbishop of Armagh: a memoir* (London, 1913).

Andrews, John, *Plantation Acres* (Belfast, 1985).

Atkinson, Edward D., *Dromore, an Ulster Diocese* (Dundalk, 1925).

Bassett, George Henry, *County Armagh 100 years ago: a guide and directory 1888* (Belfast, 1989).

Bell, J. Brian A., *A History of Garmany's Grove Presbyterian Church* (Armagh, 1970).

Burke, Bernard, *Burke's Peerage* (London, 1915).

Canavan, T., *Frontier Town, An illustrated History of Newry* (Belfast, 1989).

Close, Lilias, *The Close family in Ireland* (Hampshire, n.d.).

Coote, Charles, *Statistical survey of the county of Armagh, with observations on the means of improvement: drawn up in the years 1802, and 1803, for the consideration, and under the direction of the Dublin society* (Dublin, 1804).

Day, Angélique and McWilliams, Patrick (eds.), *Ordnance Survey Memoirs of Ireland Vol.1: Parishes of County Armagh* (Belfast, 1990).

Dean, J.A.K., *Gatelodges of Ulster* (Belfast, 1994).

Ferrar, M.L., *Register of the Royal School Armagh* (Belfast, 1933).

Fitzgerald, Desmond and Weatherup, Roger (eds.), *The way we were: historic Armagh photographs from the Allison Collection* (Belfast, 1993).

Fleming, W.E.C., *Armagh Clergy 1800-2000* (Dundalk, 2000).

Gow, Ian, 'An Architect's Melancholy' in *Irish Arts Review*, vol. 14, 1998.

Gwynn, Aubrey, *The medieval province of Armagh, 1470-1545* (Dundalk, 1946).

Hanna, Denis O'D., *The face of Ulster* (London, 1952).

Henderson, Isobel, *St. Mark's Killylea 1832–1982: A short history of Killylea parish* (Dungannon, 1982).

Hickson, Mary, *Ireland in the seventeenth century or the Irish massacres of 1641-2* (2 vols., London, 1884).

Hill, George, *An historical account of the Plantation in Ulster* (Belfast, 1877).

BIBLIOGRAPHY

Hogg, M.B., *Short History of Keady Parish: its church and its people* (Armagh, 1928).

Hughes, A.J., and Nolan, William (eds.), *Armagh history & society: interdisciplinary essays on the history of an Irish county* (Dublin, 2001).

Hughes, T., *The history of Tynan parish* (Dublin, 1910).

Kenward, James, *Prep School* (London, 1958).

Kinealy, C., and Parkhill, T. (eds.), *The Famine in Ulster* (Belfast, 1997).

Leinster-Mackay, Donald, *The Rise of the English Prep School* (1984).

Leslie, J.B., *Armagh clergy and parishes* (Dundalk, 1911).

Lewis, S., *A Topographical Dictionary of Ireland* (2 vols., London, 1837).

Lodge, John, *The Peerage of Ireland … revised …* (Dublin, 1789).

MacCarthy, R.B., *The Trinity College Estates 1800–1923* (Dundalk, 1992).

Malcomson, A.P.W., *Primate Robinson 1709-94: 'a very tough incumbent in fine preservation'* (Belfast, 2003).

Marshall, Arthur, *Whimpering in the Rhododendrons* (London, 1982).

Maxwell, I., *Researching Armagh Ancestors* (Belfast, 2000).

Maxwell, I., *Researching Down Ancestors* (Belfast, 2004).

Perceval-Maxwell, M., *The Scottish Migration to Ulster in the Reign of James I* (London, 1973).

Robinson, P., *The Plantation of Ulster* (London and Dublin, 1984).

Stuart, James, *Historical memoirs of the city of Armagh* (Newry, 1819).

Taylor, G. and Skinner, A., *Maps of the Roads of Ireland* (London and Dublin, 1777).

Temple, John, *The Irish Rebellion* (London, 1679).

Trevor, William, *Old School Ties* (London, 1976).

Weaving, Willoughby, *Poems* (London, 1913).

Weaving, Willoughby, *The Star Fields and other Poems* (Oxford, 1916).

Weaving, Willoughby, *The Bubble and other Poems*, (Oxford, 1917).

Weaving, Willoughby, *Heard Melodies*, (Oxford, 1918).

Weaving, Willoughby, *Algazel*, (London, 1920).

Weaving, Willoughby, *Deadal Wings*, (Oxford, 1920).

Weaving, Willoughby, *Ivory Palaces* (Oxford, 1931).

Weaving, Willoughby, *Spoils of Time*, (Oxford, 1934).

Weaving, Willoughby, *Toys of Eternity* (Oxford, 1937).

Weaving, Willoughby, *Purple Testament* (Oxford, 1941).

Weaving, Willoughby, *Sonnets and a few lyrics* (Abingdon-on-Thames, 1952).

Wilson, Anthony M., *A History of Mourne Grange* (1992).

INDEX

Note: references ending with 'a' denote entries relating to 'Appendix 4, Military Careers of Elm Park Headmasters'.

A Natural Approach to Mathematics, 72
'A view or an account of the lands ...', *Ashe*, 6
'Abdul Abulbul Amir', 65
Abingdon, 27, 96, 121a, 124a
Abingdon School, Oxford, 25–6, 87, 121a
Aldergrove air base, 62
'Ali Barber', *see* teaching staff, Barbour, Redmond
Anderson and McAuley Ltd, 18
Anderson, Sir Robert, 18
    Lord Mayor of Belfast, 18
'Annie Reid' *see* teaching staff, Reid, Mr
Armagh Cathedral, 74
Armagh County Museum, 14
Armagh infirmary, 63
Armagh Royal School, 2, 48
Armagh to Monaghan railway, 4
Armagh, Archbishop of, 73
Armagh, city of, 4, 40
Armagh, Dean of, *see* Maxwell, Rev. Robert
Armagh families,
    Armstrong, 24
    Brownlow, 9
    Johnston, 74
    Leslie, 24
    Speers, 97
    Stronge, 24
    Terris, 74
Armstrong, Thomas Knox, 11
Ashe, Thomas, 6
Auden, W.H., 26

'Ballynameta or Woodpark', 8,
Banchall, John, 15
BBC, 73
Beano, 31
Belfast, 18, 91, 96, 122a
Belfast News Letter, 95
Bellvue Park, Killiney, 14
Benburb, 18, 40
Blacker family, 4, 32, 59, 74, 84, 86

Blacker, Maxwell Vandeleur, *see* Blacker-Douglas, Maxwell Vandeleur
Blacker, Maxwell, (son of Grace and St.John Blacker), 9
Blacker, Rev. Samuel, 9
Blacker, Rev. St.John, 9, 12–16
Blacker, Samuel, (son of Grace and St.John Blacker), 9
Blacker, William of Carrickblacker, 9
Blacker-Douglas, Elizabeth, (wife of Blacker-Douglas, St.John), 15–16
Blacker-Douglas, Maxwell Vandeleur, (son of Grace and St.John Blacker), 12–14, 16, 18, 24
Blacker-Douglas, Robert, (son of Maxwell Blacker-Douglas), 16
    Irish Guards, 16
Blacker-Douglas, St.John, *see* Blacker, St.John
Blackwater River, 62
Bletchingley, Surrey, 118a
'Bondville or Tullybrick Etra', 8
Boulogne, 119a
'Boygen' *see* teaching staff, Fleming, Mrs Ena
Boyle, John Charters, 18–19
Boyne, 9
Brackenber House School, 51, 92, 96, 124a
Bramblestown, Co. Kilkenny, 6
Brasenose College, Oxford, 23
Bridges, Robert, 26, 121a
Browne, Misses, 8
Brownlow, Anna, (wife of Maxwell Close), 8
Buckingham, duke of, 4
Butler family, 6
Butler, Capt. James, 6
Butler, Catherine, (daughter of Dame Margaret and Capt. Butler), 6

Cabin Hill Preparatory School, 49
Calais, 118a
Campbell College, Belfast, 2, 67, 87
Campbell, John, 16
Campbell, Morris, 40

Campbell, Mrs, (wife of rector), 40
Canada, 73
Carrickblacker, 9
Carrickfergus, 120a
Carroll, James Rawson, 14
Castle Leslie, 23
Champagne, Deborah, 8
Charlemont, Lord, 8
Charlemont, second Earl of (Armstrong), 12
Charley, Robin, 26, 92
'Cheese', see James McElhinney
Chilswell, Oxford, 121a
Civil War, 5
Clark, Agnes, 15
classical schools, 1–2
Clonall, 5
Clonaule, see Clonall
Clonmacnoise, 8
Close family, 4, 32
Close, Bess, see Close, Elizabeth, (daughter of Catherine and Samuel Close)
Close, Col. Maxwell, 8–9
Close, Elizabeth, (daughter of Catherine and Samuel Close), 6–7
Close, Grace, (sister of Samuel Close), 9
Close, Margaret, (daughter of Catherine and Samuel Close), 6
Close, Maxwell, (son of Catherine and Samuel Close), 6–7
Close, Rev. Samuel, 6, 8
Close, Samuel, (son of Mary and Maxwell Close), 8–9
Clubfoot, Dr., 27
Cogrell, Robert, 15
College Hall, 5
'College Hall or Marrassit', 8
Commonwealth Society for the Blind, 23
Coote, Sir Charles, 7–8
Cork, 73
Cowdy, John, 30, 56, 72
Cox, Jane, 74, 94
Cox, Trevor, 74, 94
Craigavad, 22, 50, 120–121a, 124a
'Crearum or Fellows Hall', 8
Cremorne, Lord, 8
Crooks, Rev., Rector of Killylea, 92
Croydon, 120a
Crummit, Frank, 65
Cutteslowe, Oxford, 121a

Dame Margaret, see Maxwell, Margaret, (daughter of Margaret and Robert)
Dandy, 31
Dawson, Jemmy, 8
De Foutraine, Rev. A.H., 120a
Deane, Dr., 63, 64
Derrynoose, 40
Dieppe, 121a

Diocesan schools, 2
Donaghenry, Co. Tyrone, 6,
'Doodly' see teaching staff, McDonald, Miss
Dover, 26, 120–121a
Downpatrick, 87
Droitwich, 123a
Drumbanagher, 8–9
Drumsallen Church, 39–40
Dublin, 5

Echlin, Henry, Bishop of Down, 4
Echlin, Margaret, (daughter of Henry Echlin), 4
Eliot, T.S., 26
Elm Park, townland of, 16
Elm Park house,
    advertisement of house for sale, 6–7
    census of 1901, 15
    improvements to Elm Park, 13–14
Elm Park Prep School,
    academic standards, 67–70
        Common Entrance Exam, 1, 27, 67
        weekly tests, 68
    beech tree, 41
    boys' careers after Elm Park, 87
    closure of the school, 96
        sale of the school organ, 96
    chronological summary, 90–96
        changing fortunes, 90–91
    daily routine, 33, 36
    dairy and farm, 25
    directors of Elm Park, 73
    domestic arrangements, 59–66
        chilly weather, 65
        food and diet, 59–63
            dormitory feasts, 62
            picnics, 62
            tuck from home, 59–60
            war rationing, 59
    dormitories, 65–6
        Barnet, 29–30
        Blore Heath, 30
        Bosworth, 30
        Mortimer's Cross, 30, 92
        Northampton, 30
        St. Albans, 30
        storytelling by Weaving, 27
        Tewkesbury, 30, 64
        Towton, 30
        Wakefield, 30, 64
    entertainment, 43–5
        Elm Park Amateur Dramatic Society, 46
    First World War and Elm Park, 16
    icehouse, 32
    introduction to school life, 29–30
    living conditions, 31–2
        bullying, 31

INDEX

opening of Elm Park School, 90
parental visits, 38–9
pastimes, 30, 35–6, 40, 42
    Blue Riband contest, 46
    card games, 31
    'Charlie over the water', 35
    comics, 31
    Dinky cars, 30, 50, 62
    gardening, 46
    marbles, 30, 50
    stamp collecting, 31
sale of Elm Park, 16–17, 20
school houses, 30
    Red Rose, 30
    White Rose, 30
school population, 91–2
school uniform, 92
Second World War and Elm Park, 25, 92
sickness and childhood illnesses, 63–4, 66
    boils, 66
    chickenpox, 64
    chilblains, 66
    impetigo, 66
    measles, 64
    medical care, 65
    Minidex, 64
    Radio malt, 64
    Royal Victoria Hospital, 65
sports at Elm Park, 47–8
    athletics, 50
    cricket, 48–9, 51
        destruction of the cricket pavilion, 51
        Verity, Hedley, 49
    football, 50
    hockey, 49-50
    sports day, 50
Sundays at Elm Park, 39–41
    attendance at church, 39–40
England, 1–2, 5, 25, 49, 67–8, 91, 96, 121a
English Channel, 16
Eton collars, 92
Eton College, 2, 26

'Fairview or Mucklagh', 8
Falkland estate, Co. Monaghan, 5
Farnham estate, Co. Cavan, 5
Farnham, Baron, 6
Farnham, Lord, *see* Maxwell, John, (son of Henry Maxwell), 6
Faulkner, Baron, of Downpatrick, *see* Faulkner, Brian
Faulkner, Brian, 87
Fellows Hall, 5, 7, 11, 23, 24
'Flanders', 120a
France, 16

Gallaspie, James, 6
George V's Jubilee, 62
Gervais, Peter, 6–7
Gervaise, Bess, 8
Gilbert, Bernard, 46
Glencoe, 84
Grace Hall, Dollingstown, 13
Greer, Fanny, 15
Gregg, Primate, Archbishop of Armagh, 73
Grundt, Der Stelser, 27
Guildford, 120a

Hamilton, Alexander, (son of the Dean of Armagh), 8
Hamilton, James, 5
Hearth Money Rolls 1664, 5
Helen's Bay, 124a
Hepenstall, Ellen, 15
Heard Melodies, 26
Highgate Junior School, 26
Hill, John, 65
Holywood, 22
Hordle Poacher, The, 46
House of Commons, 2
Hughes, Kevin, 29
Hughes, Martin, 29
Hunter, Mercy, (wife of George McCann), 74

India, 123–124a
Inns of Court, 120a
Iolanthe, 46
Irish Sea, 25, 70, 91

Jacobs, W.W., 46
Joseph Orr & Sons, 18

Keady, 8
Keats, John (poet), 11
Kenward, James, 2
Kidd, Dr. William Lodge, 8–9
Kilkeel, 50, 96
Killylea, 4, 29, 31, 39, 59, 72, 87, 121–122a
Killylea church, (Church of Ireland), 39
Killylea Home Guard, 25
Killylea railway station, 11, 29, 85
Killylea, Rector of, 72, 92
Kilmore, Bishop of, *see* Echlin, Henry, Bishop of Down
King Charles II, 5
King Henry VIII, 2
King James I, 2
King James VI, 4
King, Rev. Dickie, 72
Knappagh, 39
Knappagh road, 11
Knappagh, townland of, 4–5, 74
Knockaneagh, townland of, 4
Koczeban, Mr, 84

135

Larchfield School, 26
Le Havre, 120a
Lewis, C. Day, 26
L'Herrison (The Hedgehog), 31
Limavady, Co. Londonderry, 7
Limerick, Bishop of, *see also* Owen, Mr, 40, 71
London Gazette, 121a
Lough Neagh, 96
Lowther College, 84
Luke, John, 74
Lurgan, Lord, 8
Lynch, Mary, 15

Malvern College, 23, 87
Manor House School, 49
Maxwell family, 4
Maxwell, Henry, 5–6
Maxwell, Henry, (son of James), 5
Maxwell, James, (son of James), 5
Maxwell, James, (son of Margaret and Robert), 6
Maxwell, James, (son of Robert), 5
Maxwell, John, (son of Henry Maxwell), 6
Maxwell, Lady Margaret, *see* Maxwell, Margaret, (daughter of Margaret and Robert)
Maxwell, Lieutenant James, (brother of Robert), 5
Maxwell, Margaret, (daughter of Margaret and Robert), 6–7
Maxwell, Margaret, (daughter of Robert), 5
Maxwell, Mary, (daughter of Robert Maxwell of Fellows Hall), 7
Maxwell, Phoebe, (daughter of Margaret and Robert), 6
Maxwell, Rev. Robert, 4
Maxwell, Robert, 5, 8
Maxwell, Robert, (son of Robert), 4–5
Maxwell, Sir Robert, of Orchardstown Scotland, 6
McBride and Williams Ltd, 122a
McBride, Thomas, 122a
McCall, Robert, 15
McCann, George, (husband of Mercy Hunter), 74
McClintock, Isa, 24
McClintocks, Misses, 24
McMullan, David, 62
McParlan, William, 16
  his son, John, 16
Meerut, 123a
Mitchell, Bob, 29, 48, 85, 86
Moira, Rector of, 9, *see also* Blacker, Rev. St.John
Moores of Drumbanagher, 8
Mourne Grange Preparatory School, 1, 22, 49, 50, 96
Mullabrack, Rector of, 9

'Mullach an tSionaigh', *see* Mullaghatinny
'Mullaghagherie', *see* Mullaghatinny
'Mullaghaghtelee', *see* Mullaghatinny
'Mullaghaghteny', *see* Mullaghatinny
Mullaghatinny, *see also*, Elm Park townland, 4–8, 11
Mullaghbrack, Rector of, *see* Blacker, Samuel, (son of Grace and St.John Blacker)
'Mullagh-Itynne', *see* Mullaghatinny
'Mullatinny', *see* Mullaghatinny
Murlough House, Newcastle, 22
Murray, William, 12

Newcastle-under-Lyme, 124a

Old School Ties, 94
'Olly Allport', *see* teaching staff, Allport, Robin
Omagh, 93, 123a
Orchardstown, Scotland, 6
Ordnance Survey maps, 8, 11
  mapmakers, 8
Orr, Eddie, 46
Oxford University, 22

partnership of Weaving and Seth-Smith, 22
Patterson, T.G.F., 5
Pembroke College, Oxford, 25, 121a
Pirates of Panora, The, 72, 74
placenames, 8
Plantation of Ulster, 2, 5
  Irish Plantation Measure, 6
Playfair, William, 8
poetry of Willoughby Weaving, 54–5
Porter, Jenny, 15
Poyntzpass, 8
Prep School, 2
preparatory schools, 1–2
  preparatory schools in Ulster, 22
Prime Minister of Northern Ireland, *see* Faulkner, Brian
public schools, 1–2, 67
Putty, *see* Seth-Smith, Hugh Eric

Queen Elizabeth I, 2

rebellion of 1641, 4
restoration of King Charles II, 5
Rockport Preparatory School, Criagavad, 2, 22, 49, 50, 92, 96, 120–122a, 124a
Rome, 11
Rowley, Richard, *see* Williams, R.V.
Roxborough House, Moy, 12
Royal British Legion, 124a
Royal Inniskilling Fusiliers, 92
Royal Naval College, Dartmouth, 67
Royal Schools, 2

INDEX

Sandhurst, 124a
'School magazine', 65
Scott, Mr, (Killylea railway station master), 29
Sedburgh, 87
See Rental of 1631, 5
See Rental of 1676, 5
Seth-Smith, Charles Edward, (father of Hugh Eric Seth-Smith), 120a
Seth-Smith, Florence née Stevenson, (mother of Hugh Eric Seth-Smith), 120a
Seth-Smith, Grace, 23
Seth-Smith, Hugh Eric, 18, 22–7, 29, 31, 33, 38, 40, 44, 49, 59, 64, 71, 73, 84–7, 91–3, 96, 120–122a, 124a
    attitude to discipline, 23–4
    death of, 20, 92–3
    education, 23
    family eye disorder, 23
    military career, 22–3, 120–121a
    motorcycle and sidecar, 22
    pet dogs,
        Clodagh, 24
        Fuss, 24
        Puck, 24
        Timoshenko, 24
Seth-Smith, Muriel, 23
Setty, *see* Seth-Smith, Hugh Eric
Sewell, Ernest, 46
Shelley, Percy Bysshe, 12
Shrewsbury Public School, 87
Silvermere, Cobham, Surrey, 23, 25
Southampton, 120a
'Spitzboygen', *see* teaching staff, Fleming, Mrs Ena
SS *Dieppe*, 120a
St Columba's College, Dublin, 2, 67, 87
St Patrick, 48
St Margaret's Mansions, 120a
staff at Elm Park,
    non-teaching staff, 84
        Acheson, Yvonne, 84
        Bleakley, Willy, 86
        Bruce, Cecil, 85
        Connelly, Alfie, 85
        Cranston, Miss, 84
        Kerr, Thomas, 16, 86
        Knipe, Jimmy, 86
        Koczeban, Mr, 84
        Leader, Miss Patience, 84
        Linton, John, 16, 74
            his son, John, 16
        Lutton, Joseph, 86
        Mair, Miss, 84
        McDonald, Miss, 84
        McDowell, Miss, 84
        McElhinney, James, 86
        McIlveen, James, 85
        MeGaw, Miss, 84, 93
        Nutter, Miss, 84
        Rocks, John, 86
        Sewell, Miss Phyllis, 84
        Seymour, Miss, 84, 90
        Shea, Miss Molly, 84, 92, 93, 124a
    household staff, 85–6
        maids, 85
        matrons, 84
    outdoor staff and farm workers, 85–6
    teaching staff, 71–4
        art class, 74
        carpentry class, 74
        discipline, 74
            'little Jacob', 74
        headmasters, 71
        music class, 74
        schoolteachers
            Allport, Robin, 72, 74, 93
            Baker, Esau, 74
            Baker, Jacob, 74
            Baker, Mr Redmond, 56, 72
            Breeze, Mr, 94
            Britten, Mr C.D., 72
            Bronwell, Miss, 84
            Brownell, Miss, 32, 93
            Burrows, Miss, 73
            Clayton, Mr Harold, 72, 74
            Coleman, Mr E.W., 71
            Emerson, Miss, 93
            Fanning, Miss, 71
            Farley, Vernon, 72, 74
            ffrench-Eager, Miss, 93
            Fleming, Mrs Ena, 60, 72–3, 84, 93
            Forge, G.B., 71
            Foster, Miss, 72
            Hanbury, Mr Brian, 93
            Hannon, David, 73, 93
                television producer with BBC, 73
            Harris, Mr, 93
            Hodgett, Dick, 74
            Hunter-Blair, Mr J.W., 71
            Irwin, Miss, 71
            Lowdell, George, 73, 93
            McCordock, Miss, 74
            McEndoo, Miss Leslie, 73–4
            McQuaid, Miss, 93
            Nesbitt, Miss, 93
            Nichols, Mr Norman, 93
            Oliver, Miss, 72
            Owen, Mr E., 40, 71
            Parkinson, Miss, 93
            Reid, Mr, 74
            Sewell, Miss, 60, 73
            Sharpley, Mr E.N., 50, 72
            Shea, Miss, 32
            Simpson, Jack, 74

Simpson, Miss, 73
Vaughan, Mr G.R., 94
West, Reginald, 74
Willans, Mr G.A., 72
staff changes, 93–4
Statistical Survey of the County of Armagh, 8
Strachan, David, 39
Summer Fields, 26
'Sunlit trees in late autumn', 54-5
Sutty, *see* Seth-Smith, Hugh Eric

Taylor and Skinner map, 11
TCD, *see* Trinity College Dublin
Temple, Sir William, 5
The Downs, Colwall, 26
The Glen, 32, 53–57, 60, 85
  birdkeeping, 57
  nature walks, 54
  swimming, 54
  tree houses, 56–7
    Cowdy house, 56
    Guam, 56
    Herdman house, 57
    Midway, 56
    Tobruk, 56
'the invention', 86
Tonnagh, townland of, 4, 11, 53
Townland Valuation of 1830s, 9
Toys of Eternity, 55
Trevor, William, *see also* Cox, Trevor, 74
Trimblestown Cottage, Co. Dublin, 12
Trinac, 35, 63
Tri-Nac, *see* Trinac
Trinacia, *see* Trinac
Trinity College Dublin, 2, 4–5, 92–3, 122a, 124a
'Tubby' Clayton, *see* teaching staff, Clayton, Harold
Tullahennel estate, Co. Kerry, 12
Tynan, 4, 8–9
Tynan Abbey, 23

university, 1
Usher, Primate Henry, 4

Vinecash, Portadown, 74

Ward, Cyril, 60, 62
Warming Pan, The, 46
Wars of the Roses, 30, *see also* Elm Park, school houses
Weaving, Beatrice Anne née Armitage, (mother of Willoughby Weaving), 121a
Weaving, Harry Walker, (father of Willoughby Weaving), 121a
Weaving, Harry Willoughby, 18, 22, 24–7, 29, 31, 38, 40, 46, 49, 54, 59, 67, 73, 87, 91–6, 120–124a
  education, 25–6
  literary achievements, 26
  military career, 26, 121–122a
  retirement 27, 96
  teaching style, 27
Weaving, Montague, 73, 92–3, 124a
  death of, 93
Wellington, South India, 123a
Westminster, London, 22, 120a
Whelan, Elisa, 15
Williams, Allan, (brother of Michael Williams), 122a
Williams, Barbara, (sister of Michael Williams), 122a
Williams, Betty, (sister of Michael Williams), 122a
Williams, Joan, (sister of Michael Williams), 122a
Williams, Margaret Sophie née Pollock, (mother of Michael Williams), 92, 122a
Williams, Michael Valentine Rowley, 26, 71, 73, 84, 92, 93, 96
  military awards, 124a
  military career, 122–124a
    Burma campaign, 123a
      Arakan, 123a
      Bengal, 123a
      Chittagong, 123a
      Comilla, 123a
      Delhi, 123a
      Deolali, 124a
      Jullundur, 123a
      Feni, 123a
      Kyaukpandowrma, 123a
      Lahore, 123a
      Punjab, 123a
      Yenangyaung, 123a
Williams, Rowley Valentine, (father of Michael Williams), 26, 92, 120a, 122a
Willow, *see* Weaving, Harry Willoughby
Wilton Terrace, Belgravia, 23
Woolley, Charles, 6
Wreckin College, 92, 122a

Yates, Dornford, 27